Praise for

I'm God's Daughter

Captivating, courageous, and liberating are three facets that come to mind when I think of Kanisha Parker's latest devotional, *I'm God's Daughter*. Kanisha fearlessly addresses a taboo subject, spiritual abuse, tackling it with God's gentleness, care, and, most importantly, love. The devotional intertwined her testimony while encouraging us all to remember that God is all we need and more.

I'm God's Daughter is beautifully written with God's daughters in mind. Because of this, I believe readers will sense God's presence on every page. Reading the devotional reminded me that God sees, knows, and cares about us even during trying circumstances, which made me smile and helped me understand God's love for me even more.

Every woman needs to read Kanisha's devotional for such a time as this. It's a beautiful masterpiece. It will lead you on a path of self-discovery, deepen your connection with God, and encourage you to give God all your worries, anxieties, and cares. Include this indispensable devotional to accompany you on a sixty-day journey brimming with revelation, testimonies, and the word of God!

Candace Writes, minister, psychotherapist, and author of *Breathe: Rest, Reflect, Reset,* and *Woman of God: 60-Day Devotional*

I'm God's Daughter is a needed devotional for such a time as this. In a world where women are daily faced with wrong-headed cultural messaging about our identities, we must lean into the Truth of who we truly are. Kanisha's personal experience and passion with this subject matter shines through and will make readers feel seen on even their darkest days.

Ericka Andersen, author of *Reason to Return: Why Women Need the Church and the Church Needs Women*

As a daughter of world-renowned leaders, I am very familiar with both the advantages and disadvantages of being their daughter. So I think it not strange at all that to accept Christ and be God's daughter would come with the same disadvantages and advantages. This devotional will help you to find your way in handling being a daughter—and not just find your way but enhance the tools and relationships you have with God as a Father. It's not easy being God's daughter but resources like this devotional make it easier. I encourage you to go deeper in your heart to heart with God. Grab this devotional and awaken the daughter of God even the more in you.

Pastor Cora Jakes, The Potter's House of Dallas

This book is literally a transformative guide to finding who you are in Christ. For a lot of Christian women, we've experienced some really unbiblical and hurtful things in our home church that cause a lot of baggage and unclarity (in all areas). This book is a catalyst to healing, discovery, and WINNING as a Christian woman! If you're exploring your identity, healing from anything, and want to step into who God wants you to be, the book is a must-have!

Brandi Chew, CMO of BrandIt Strategies and founder of *ChurchGrow*

I am a proponent of deliverance, but I am further a proponent of having realistic ways that help and assist us in staying delivered. For far too long there have been many instances where the topic of deliverance has been discussed within the church, but no real wisdom is shared on practical, realistic ways to help individuals walk out their deliverance daily. This devotion and the testimony behind it points all who will read it to a place of active deliverance and being able to stay delivered. Also, while being empowered, affirmed, and validated as the Daughter of God we were always intended to be!

Author Kanisha Parker has produced a life-changing, powerful and courageous devotion that will bless millions of women whose story identifies with hers and even those whose stories may not. The sole purpose of understanding that we are God's Daughters is to know that no matter what we've been through in life, and no matter how ugly our story may seem to be, God has a way of taking that same ugly story and making it into a beautiful testimony that displays God's ability to change us, transform us, and make us beautiful, whole, and healed Daughters of God.

Evangelist Nicole A. Alston, Missouri Midwest Ecclesiastical Jurisdiction COGIC

I'm God's Daughter

60 Days of Discovering Who God Says You
Are and Who He Wants You to Be

BY KANISHA PARKER

Published by KHARIS PUBLISHING, an imprint of
KHARIS MEDIA LLC.

Copyright © 2024 Kanisha Parker

ISBN-13: 978-1-63746-256-0

ISBN-10: 1-63746-256-5

Library of Congress Control Number: 2024934225

All KHARIS PUBLISHING products are available at special quantity discounts for bulk purchase for sales promotions, premiums, fund-raising, and educational needs. For details, contact:

Kharis Media LLC
Tel: 1-630-909-3405
support@kharispublishing.com
www.kharispublishing.com

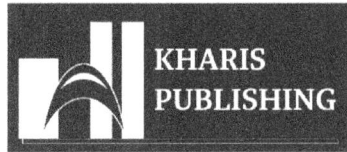

KHARIS
PUBLISHING

To every daughter of God, let this be your reminder

that you have always been His.

CONTENTS

PROLOGUE

I grew up extremely sheltered. From the age of 10, all I knew was church. Everyone at school considered me a "holy roller." My siblings, cousins, and I weren't allowed to go to parties, prom, or most social events outside of church, and were discouraged from having friends who didn't go to our church. Beyond being overprotected, we were cut off from our extended family and the rest of the world, all in the name of "living holy." My mom, a single mother who wanted to protect us from all she'd seen and suffered in her own life, thought she'd found a safe place in our church and in the man who led it. Every aspect of our lives was overseen by his teachings, opinions, and control.

At the time, I thought this was normal and appropriate. It's what we were taught. No alternative perspective had been presented to me as an option. Moreover, no one at church openly questioned or opposed our way of life. Simply put, I didn't know any better, and with no point of reference outside the four walls of our church, I remained loyal for nearly 20 years.

The same man I called "Bishop" was the same man who groomed me for years, taking advantage of my naïveté, low self-esteem, and longing for acceptance. The same man I considered a father figure drove a wedge between me and my mother, my sisters, and the rest of my family. The same man who taught me about God was the same man who manipulated me into giving up my virginity and coerced me into a secret life of sexual sin during my early 20s. He was twice my age.

It wasn't until I was 30 years old, three years after his death, that I moved away from home for a fresh start in Dallas, Texas. There, it was just me and God. With no distractions from the pain of my past, emotions I'd tucked away or simply didn't understand began making their way to the surface. I had just started dating my now husband, Xavier, and we were in a long-distance relationship. Although my ability to be transparent with him about my past gave me the confidence that he would be my husband one day, I still found it difficult to fully let my guard down and allow him to love me because I didn't trust men. Fortunately, he was patient with me, accepting of my past, and willing to remain with me for the journey of healing still to come. He had been in therapy for years and encouraged me to seek the help I needed to understand the past trauma that was hindering my present life.

While I was now free from the toxic environment I grew up in, it took months to come to terms with who I was as a result of the previous 20 years of my life, to tear down the lies I had accepted as truth and begin the process of rebuilding.

In November 2021, I started going to therapy to unpack all those years of what I now understood was spiritual abuse and religious trauma. Learning and accepting the truth of what happened to me unlocked the door to true healing and freedom—a healing and freedom I needed to confront my past so I could become the wife and mother I was destined to be, and so I could finally share my story with girls and women who needed to hear it.

I started writing this book in 2019, when I was just beginning to embark on my personal journey of self-discovery, and I didn't finish it until 2023. I'd finally reached the other side of that long journey back to who God created me to be and always knew I was: His daughter.

I'm God's Daughter is the book I needed at the age of 14, when my life was radically altered by spiritual abuse and coercion. While I wish I'd had a book that told me who I was so I wouldn't spend half my life trying to figure it out, I also know that what I initially saw as 20 years of wasted time and trauma, was never wasted to God. Though the enemy meant those decades as evil against me, God meant them for the good, and gave me a powerful testimony that will be a way out, a way through, and a way over for someone else. He makes all things new, and I know the beautiful life I have today is only a testament to His infinite grace, mercy, and love towards me.

This is the book I'll give to my own daughter when she approaches that age of discovery, to both inform and remind her of who and whose she is before the enemy's lies try to convince her otherwise.

It's the book I've written for you, a fellow daughter of God, to affirm you, uplift you, and redirect you back to your Creator, the One who loves and adores you just the way you are.

Maybe your story's just beginning. Or maybe you're starting anew. Either way, I want you to know that your identity is rooted in His truth—His word—and I pray this book will guide you to think, believe, and embrace who He says you are, allowing Him to govern your life's decisions by His design.

Knowledge truly is power. With the knowledge of what it means to be a daughter of God, I believe you'll be prepared to cast down any thought that challenges this truth: He is yours, and you are His.

This one radical realization changes *everything*.

INTRODUCTION

Finally, brothers and sisters, whatever is true, whatever is noble, whatever is right, whatever is pure, whatever is lovely, whatever is admirable—if anything is excellent or praiseworthy—think about such things. Whatever you have learned or received or heard from me, or seen in me—put it into practice. And the God of peace will be with you.

Philippians 4:8-9, NIV

SCRIPTURE

Just like this introduction, each chapter of *I'm God's Daughter* begins with Scripture because the Word of God is our foundation. The Word grounds, affirms and directs us. As a daughter of God, it's important to get into the habit of turning to the Word rather than the world for the blueprint of how we should think and act. To know and understand who you are, you have to seek clarity from the One who made you.

DEVOTIONAL

Every devotion stems from Philippians 4:8-9, which tells us how we should frame our thoughts. This matters because our thoughts dictate our actions and therefore our character and identity. Every thought that comes to your mind does not belong to you. Because Satan cannot force you to sin, he sends thoughts to try to get you off track and outside of the will of God for your life. But God has given us the Holy Spirit to guide us into mindful, prosperous action. Our thinking is the vehicle by which we become more like Christ, execute the purpose He created us to pursue, and obtain the things God has planned for us. By carefully choosing the thoughts we meditate on, we gain control over our minds and our actions, and eliminate the enemy's ability to use our thoughts against us. Every devotion is geared towards teaching you to think clearly and truthfully about God, yourself, and others, so you can be the image bearer God created you to be.

REFLECTION

The Word of God says that death and life are in the power of your tongue (Proverbs 18:21). Thoughts matter, but so does using your voice to speak life over yourself. Use this time and space to come out of agreement with the lies of the enemy and into agreement with God's truth.

PRAYER

Last, seal each day with prayer and expectation, believing that God will honor the time you've invested in getting to know Him better, and that He will grant you the desires of your heart.

◆◆◆

God put you on this earth for a purpose—to be a witness of the redeeming power of Christ and to bring glory to His name. Know that purpose far outweighs any poor decision, wrong turn, or mistake you've ever made.

As you embark on this journey, keep in mind that growth is messy! You won't always get it right. You won't always feel like putting forth the effort, and you certainly won't always enjoy the process. But every step you take toward knowing God better is worthwhile. Becoming more like Christ in the way we think and act is a lifelong process—and it all begins with examining our thoughts.

I'm God's Daughter will teach you what God truly thinks and feels about you and, as a result, you will begin to expect the best from God and yourself. You will approach situations differently because you want to please Him. You will learn who you are as a daughter of God and how to respond in a way that reflects your God-given identity. Doing so means you must realize and recognize not only who you are, but who you are *not*, which will radically transform how you think and speak about yourself.

And that, daughter of God, requires that you know *the truth*.

WHATEVER IS TRUE

Reject the lies. Embrace the truth.

The first thing Paul tells us to think about in Philippians 4:8 is things that are true. When you think about something, you are focusing or reflecting on a certain thought, concept, or idea for an extended period of time. In his list of things to think about, it's no coincidence that Paul first encourages us to dwell on the truth, because that's exactly what God's Word is: the Truth. In order to embrace it, we must reject the enemy's lies.

God wants His Truth to become your foundation. When a foundation is strong and sure, it cannot be moved by any storm, attack, or obstacle. When your thoughts are founded on the Truth—the very Word of God and what God says about you—the lies the enemy constantly attempts to feed your mind can no longer stand. But when you do not know, believe, and live by the Truth, you accept the enemy's lies as fact, and therefore you may act upon the false narrative Satan has concocted to divert you from the will of God.

Satan surreptitiously feeds us countless lies that make us *feel* as though we are neither loved by, nor important to God, nor worthy of the blessings a relationship with Him provides. When we let these lies torment our minds, we are left with a distorted view of ourselves and the way God sees us. When you recognize how the lies of the enemy are operating in your life, you can take back your power by identifying and standing on the Truth. As you fully embrace the truth of what God says about you, no lie of the enemy can stop you.

The truth is, Satan has absolutely no power over you, which is why he sends lies and negativity to encapsulate you in a state of fear, anxiety, resentment, anger, bitterness, sadness, and doubt. These defeatist mindsets are strongholds that will debilitate you and prevent you from moving forward in God—but the power of God can tear down every single one of those mindsets.

In this section, we will uncover 15 truths God says about you. Knowing these truths gives you a bold confidence no one can take away from you. God's Word is the Truth, and all throughout the Bible we can discover the truth about who we are in God and our rights as His daughters. When you build your life on a foundation of truth, you will not be deterred by any difficulty, threat, or lie.

Your situation does not define you. Your occupation does not define you. Your past, your family history, your diagnosis—none of these factors have the ability or the right to define you when you know who you are in God.

It doesn't matter what my circumstance says.

It doesn't matter what anyone else thinks or says about me.

It doesn't even matter how I feel at this moment.

My feelings must line up with the Word of God, because I am who God says I am.

I Am His

The Father has loved us so much that we are called children of God. And we really are his children. The reason the people in the world do not know us is that they have not known him.

1 John 3:1, NCV

Have you ever felt out of place or as though you simply do not belong? You search high and low for someone to accept, understand, and love you for who you are, but keep coming up empty-handed. You long to belong and to be loved for who you are without having to conform to someone else's standard. You want to find your place, your people, your tribe, and wonder if anyone will ever embrace the real you.

Just because you share a last name with someone does not mean you feel like you belong. Just because you're in a room full of people does not mean you feel welcome. Just because you've known a person all of your life does not mean you feel safe or at home around them. No matter who we are or where we come from, we all have a natural desire for a sense of belonging and security.

This desire for belonging is not strange or wrong; every human has an innate and God-given longing for love and acceptance. We want to find where we "fit," which is what causes us to gravitate towards individuals who show us attention and make us feel that we matter to them. Still, there are times when it can feel like you don't fit in, don't belong, and don't have anyone who will receive you and all of the unique qualities and characteristics you bring to the table. A lack of acceptance leads to feelings of rejection and inadequacy that make you believe there's something wrong with you, but there isn't. Everyone deserves to be loved, respected, and shown genuine, unconditional affection and attention.

Problems arise when we seek to satisfy our need for belonging in the company of the wrong people. When the enemy sees a lack of acceptance in your life that hinders you from being the real you, he will strategically place people in your life to capitalize on your weaknesses and insecurities. It is Satan's mission to keep you from ever recognizing that you *do* belong: to God.

Even if no one else welcomes you with open arms, you can rest assured that God has His arms open wide to accept you. He made you, and you are His. He wants you to know that He is your Father, friend, and greatest supporter. We won't always feel loved or accepted by people, but we can always be confident that God will never discard or dismiss us.

You are a daughter of the Most High King, which means you have rights. You have a right to love, happiness, success, peace, joy, freedom, fulfillment, and so much more: simply because you are *His*. You are not a failure or a mistake. You are His. And He loves you, just for who you are.

Reflect and Pray

I reject the lie that I do not belong. I embrace the truth that I belong to God and I am accepted and welcomed by Him.

Lord, thank You for loving and accepting me for who I am. Thank You for reminding me that I belong to You. Thank You for giving me my true identity and receiving me with open arms. I am Yours forever.

In Jesus' name, Amen.

I Am Loved

So we know the love that God has for us, and we trust that love. God is love. Everyone who lives in love lives in God, and God lives in them.

1 John 4:16, ERV

"Nobody loves me." This despairing thought comes when you feel like no one in your life shows you authentic, unconditional care, concern, and appreciation – and it hurts. It hurts when you love people and they don't love you in return. It hurts when you shower someone with affection and their response is harsh or dismissive. You are left with a hollow feeling that leads you to chase after love in people, material possessions, the hustle for "success," or sinful habits. When you don't feel loved, what you really want is to be *fulfilled*, something that we should first and foremost seek in the arms of God.

God's love *fills* you and *fulfills* you: His love *consumes* and *completes* you. His love will not leave you empty and His well never runs dry. The void you have for love and total acceptance must be filled by God. Allow God to show you how much He genuinely loves you, with no strings attached. You don't have to do anything to receive this love; it's already yours. You will never find anyone who will love you like God loves you.

The lie that no one loves you is a trick the enemy uses all the time. When you fail to realize that you are loved, you don't feel important or valued. You then become so thirsty for attention that you accept it however it comes, and the enemy will strategically use people to show you *feigned* affection and attention that make you think they love you when they really don't. They are merely in your life to distract you from drawing closer to God. Chasing after love in dead-end destinations results in self-destructive habits that push you away from God when you should be gravitating towards Him.

Even when people do love us and mean well, when we prioritize their love and place in our lives above God's, we have made them idols. We can't allow people (or things) to occupy first place in our lives—that position belongs to God.

Always be careful to guard yourself against predators—people who don't love you and are only in your life to take advantage of and deter you. When you receive God's love, He will also bless you with the right people in your life: friends and mentors who genuinely love and support you. Don't let your heart be so hardened by disappointment and rejection that you become reluctant to trust them with your vulnerability when God has them in your life to help you.

Remember that God *is* love. He doesn't have to *make* Himself love you, even when you make a mistake. Because God *is* love, He *always* loves. So know that you are, always have been, and always will be loved by God. The next time you feel unloved, go to God first. He wants to wrap you in His loving arms and show you that His love is vaster and more eternal than the love another person can give. You can't even love yourself as much as God loves you. When we fully receive and depend on God's love for us, we will be able to love ourselves and others the way we should: wholly and unconditionally.

Reflect and Pray

I reject the lie that no one loves me or that I am not worthy of love. I embrace the truth that God loves me completely and unconditionally.

Lord, thank You for loving me so passionately and relentlessly. Thank You for loving me beyond my mistakes and shortcomings and for reassuring me that I am loved by You. No longer will I search for love when I know that all the love I'll ever need is found first and foremost in You.

In Jesus' name, Amen.

I Am Cared About

Casting all your cares [all your anxieties, all your worries, and all your concerns, once and for all] on Him, for He cares about you [with deepest affection, and watches over you very carefully].

1 Peter 5:7, AMP

Care is: concern *expressed*. When you care about someone, you pay attention to them and do what you can to show up for, support, and help them. You notice when something is wrong and do what you can to assist them. You desire and pray for them to be happy, healthy, and successful. Sometimes when people don't show this loving, concerned attention towards you, it can *feel* as though no one cares about how you're doing. Fortunately, you can always be sure of this one thing: God cares about you.

We're all only human—there will be times others don't recognize your needs because they're dealing with what's going on in their own lives. It takes grace and maturity to be understanding when this happens. Still, when you truly care about someone, it moves you to put your own needs aside in order to show them that you are thinking about them and their well-being matters to you. If we want others to care about us, we should also remember to extend this expression of sincere concern toward them.

On the other hand, sometimes people authentically care about you and are doing everything they can to show it, yet Satan will still trick you into believing they don't. He tries to get you to compare what you've done for them to what they've done for you and see their level of caring as insufficient. He might convince you to compare your relationships to ones you see on social media; then you start to entertain the idea that their family and friends care about them more than yours do about you. This cycle of comparison is destructive and pointless, because regardless of which side of the spectrum you find yourself on, God cares for you.

The truth is: God is *concerned* about you. He takes a deep interest in whatever is hurting, frightening, stressing, or bothering you. He wants to share your successes, carry your burdens, and restore the joy that is lost in the midst of your most troubling times. He wants to know every difficult, hurtful, or painful thought on your mind and not only that, but He wants to take them from you. God loves you so much that He does not want you to be worried, stressed, perplexed, or confused. He did not create you to worry—He created you to *trust and rely on Him* and to relax in the true and comforting thought that your Father cares about you too much to let you worry about things He's already taken care of.

God is the Good Shepherd, and the last thing He wants is for you, his sheep, to feel like He is not everything you need—and more. Not feeling cared about is a distressing state of mind, but your Shepherd wants you to be at peace. He wants you to relinquish all of your concerns to Him.

When you give God all of your worries and cares, the peace of God washes over you in the most calming way. It is His spirit reassuring you that He is with you, He is watching, He is in control, and He cares.

Reflect and Pray

I reject the lie that I am not cared about. I embrace the truth that God cares for, is concerned about, and is always thinking of me.

Lord, thank You for caring for, covering, and protecting me. I will put my complete trust in Your plan, knowing that You will not fail or abandon me. Thank You for taking care of me and everything that concerns me as I rest safely in Your will.

In Jesus' name, Amen.

I Am Valuable

Or do you not know that your body is a temple of the Holy Spirit within you, whom you have from God? You are not your own, for you were bought with a price. So glorify God in your body.

1 Corinthians 6:19-20, ESV

Worthless.

This offensive, hurtful, and paralyzing insult carries so much weight. If you've ever felt or been called worthless, you know how deeply this hopeless and disheartening *lie* can affect you, but it goes against everything the Word of God says about you.

Do you know that your value can never be diminished nor depreciated, no matter what you do or what happens to you?

Not knowing you are valuable gives the enemy an open door into your life, which allows him to persuade you into believing your value has decreased. He will torment you with what happened to you in your past or tempt you to sin and fall short of the glory of God. His ultimate goal is to make you *feel* like you've lost value because of your failures or the transgressions committed against you so you will give up on pursuing a relationship with God. When we sin, we are left with shame, guilt, and condemnation that weigh us down and generate a fear that there is no hope for redemption. Without repenting and pursuing transformation, we are held hostage to our past mistakes and become buried in feelings of worthlessness and regret.

In those times when we feel our value has been tainted because of sins others committed against us, we shouldn't carry the blame. Don't allow shame to rob you of a hopeful, prosperous present and future, despite the ugly, horrible things that happened to you in your past. It is not your fault, and it does not have to be the end of your story.

The truth is: we are *never* viewed as less valuable in the sight of God because of our actions or what we've experienced. Furthermore, God sees all sins the same: no sin is worse than the next. These deeds make us feel so worthless and ashamed that just like Adam and Eve hid themselves from God when they disobeyed Him in the Garden, we try to cover our shame and allow it to push us away from the One we should be running to. God lovingly chases after and convicts us so we will face ourselves and return to a right relationship with Him. Because of the love and forgiveness of God towards us, we have every right to reclaim our value, which was never diminished or lost.

You cannot buy, sell, or trade your value. Still, we sometimes try to find our value in things and people and are met with disappointment and emptiness. Your value does not come from your family, friends, occupation, or possessions. You are valuable because God says you are, and because you are a daughter of God. No person, thing, or deed can make you any more or less valuable to Him. When you know *who* and *whose* you are, nothing and no one can take this God-given power of self away from you. Your value comes from God, and when you acquire your value in Christ, it won't matter what anyone else says or thinks about you because you recognize they don't have the power to define or confine you.

God paid the price for you by sending Jesus Christ to die for your sins, making you worthy of His grace, mercy, and forgiveness. You cannot do anything to make yourself worthy of what God has done and continues to do for you. Know your worth and honor and respect yourself to show God that you don't take His sacrificial love for granted.

Reflect and Pray

I reject the lie that I am worthless or useless. I embrace the truth that I am valuable and nothing can change or diminish that. My worth and identity are rooted in Christ.

Lord, thank You that my value can never be taken from me. Thank You, Jesus, for humbling Yourself and bearing the weight of my sin and deeming me worthy of Your love, grace, mercy, and forgiveness. I will cherish my value and reject every thought and decision that compromises my true worth.

In Jesus' name, Amen.

1 Am Chosen

You did not choose me; I chose you. And I gave you this work: to go and produce fruit, fruit that will last. Then the Father will give you anything you ask for in my name.

John 15:16, NCV

Have you ever felt like some people have a greater purpose in God than you do? It's easy to look at preachers, pastors, ministers, worship leaders, and others, and think they are clearly chosen by God because their gifts are so visible. Have you ever thought to yourself, *what about me? Am I chosen?* Or, have you ever asked yourself, *why would God choose me?*

Jesus says in Matthew 22:14, "For many are called, but few are chosen" (KJV). To be called simply means God created you with a purpose and a plan for your life that He wants you to accomplish. Answering God's call with your surrender is what makes you *chosen.*

The enemy's job is to prevent you from answering the call and walking in the bold confidence of being chosen by God. He wants you to believe the lie that your mistakes have disqualified you from being used by God. He wants you to think your gifts are inferior, or that you have little to nothing to offer the Kingdom of God.

God does not choose perfect people. He does not choose based on outward appearance. He does not choose those who seem qualified, advanced, or "worthy" of being used by Him to draw others to Christ. He loves to choose unlikely, imperfect people who are overlooked by others, because it yields an even greater glory to God when you are successful. God wants to use you to prove to others that nothing is impossible with Him. God already chose and qualified you. By choosing Him in return, you are making the decision to accept the call and follow God's will.

Being chosen gives you the comfort of knowing you have an important position in the Kingdom of God. God has chosen you to fulfill a divine and unique purpose on this Earth and He is counting on you to see it through. Trust that God knows, loves, and sees you for who you are. His mercy won't fail you and His promises are yours for the taking! As long as you stay in step with Him, you will accomplish and obtain everything God predestined for you to achieve.

Since you are chosen, you have the right to reject any mindset, person, or distraction that beckons you to believe otherwise. Don't settle for second rate when you've been chosen for God's best. Don't resist the tug of God's calling on your life just because it requires discipline and sacrifice. You are more than able to complete this mission. God chose you because He knows you have what it takes. He knows you will not stop or quit when the going gets tough. Everyone won't stand with you but God is undergirding you and endowing you with every tool you need for His will to be manifested in your life.

That gift you're sitting on, that calling you're afraid to fully step into – it's time to surrender and allow God to use you. You can do this because you are backed by an incomparable God who never has and never will be defeated. Hold your head up high, put your shoulders back, and step forward on the path of greatness that God has already prepared for you. You've been chosen by the Lord your God and you will accomplish this mission.

Reflect and Pray

I reject the lie that I am not good enough or too broken to be used by God. I embrace the truth that I am called and chosen to do great things for the Kingdom of God.

Lord, thank You for choosing me to do a great work for You. Thank You for believing in me enough to anoint and allow me to fulfill Your purpose in this world. I humble myself completely to You and bless Your holy name for everything You've done and are going to do with my life.

In Jesus' name, Amen.

I Am Forgiven

*If we confess our sins, he is faithful and just to forgive us our sins
and to cleanse us from all unrighteousness.*

1 John 1:9, TLB

Have you ever wronged someone, apologized, and reconciled with them? The person said they forgave you, but later reminded you of what you did to them?

Thankfully, this is never the case when you ask God forgiveness. When He forgives you, it is forever. Your sins are no longer on His mind because He doesn't want anything to separate you from His love, and that's what sin does. It separates us from enjoying a close, loving, and fulfilling relationship with God, our Father. Man does not always have the desire or capacity to forgive and forget, but God does.

Psalm 103:8-9 says God is "merciful and tender toward those who don't deserve it; he is slow to get angry and full of kindness and love. He never bears a grudge, nor remains angry forever" (TLB). Yet the enemy wants us to believe the contrary: that God is still mad at us for our sins and doesn't want to hear what we have to say. God is not interested in dwelling on your sins. He wants to have a relationship with you and bless you tremendously, so the last thing He's going to do is prevent you from getting closer to Him.

The enemy will torment you with painful reminders of what you did, hoping to get you to focus so much on your wrong that you don't accept God's forgiveness. But God forgets about your sins because He wants *you* to forget about them and move on with your life. Your mistakes have no power when they are covered in the gracious blood of Jesus Christ. God doesn't want your wrongdoings to hold you back from enjoying the abundant life He promised you in Christ Jesus.

Forgive means to grant pardon of an offense. We know God is hurt and offended when we sin, but He also sees *beyond* our wrong because He knows our hearts. As our loving Father, God sent His Son Jesus to die on the cross, bearing the burden of our sins and giving us the gift of the Holy Spirit, our keeper, to help us resist the urge to sin. That's why He's disappointed when we give in to sin rather than fight against the temptation that entices us away from Him. Our salvation secures us a right relationship with God, but unaddressed sin pushes us out of His presence.

No loving Father would want to be separated from His child, and that is how God feels about you. He wants you to cling to Him and dwell in His presence always. When you admit your faults to God, He immediately forgives you. If there is anything lingering, don't let shame keep you away from your Maker. It doesn't matter what you've done, God is just waiting for you to come back to Him. He in no way condemns or hates you. He wants to restore you, shower you with grace, and show you how His plan is undoubtedly superior to anything you could try to do on your own.

Your past mistakes are irrelevant when you've been forgiven by God, so let confession grant you access to the freedom God sacrificed His Son Jesus for you to have.

Reflect and Pray

I reject the lie that God does not love me anymore because I messed up. I embrace the truth that God is full of kindness and love and will always forgive me of my sins.

Lord, thank You for being eager to forgive me and cleanse me from all of my sins. Thank You for Your constant willingness to show me compassionate grace and mercy that I do not deserve. I will walk in the truth that You have forgiven me and I have been changed.

In Jesus' name, Amen.

I Am Free

Therefore if the Son makes you free, you shall be free indeed.

John 8:36, NKJV

Shame. Guilt. Despair. Regret. Depression. Fear. Anxiety. Heaviness.

These are mental, emotional, and spiritual *weights*: side effects of sin. Sometimes that sin isn't your own, but is a generational curse, or an unwanted result of what someone else did to you. These weights pull you down, rendering you ineffective in the kingdom of God. They keep you stuck in a cycle of defeat that looks nothing like the life God desires and planned for you to have.

God wants you to be *free*. Free from your past. Free from negative mindsets. Free from the traps. Free from the residual, lasting, and detrimental effects of sin. That is why He sent Jesus Christ to be crucified, and to rise again—so that the enemy wouldn't be able to use sin to wield control over you.

Freedom is your God-given right as a child of God, and when you're free, nothing can stop you. You can do and be anything. You will soar because nothing is weighing you down or holding you back anymore. It doesn't mean you won't face troubles or difficulties—you will—but you will also successfully overcome every obstacle. Your past or family history cannot stop you from walking in the fullness of who God called you to be.

The enemy's job is to bind you mentally, spiritually, emotionally, or physically in order to prevent you from being everything God wants and created you to be. He tries to get you to constantly dwell on your past mistakes, hurts, and disappointments. If you don't take authority over your mind by speaking God's truth over your life, Satan will oppress you so heavily that all you'll want to do is wallow in the shame and guilt of what you did or what someone did to you. He wants you to believe the lie that your past denies you the right to do God's will and obtain everything God said is yours. He wants you to get stuck in the murky waters of self-pity, and to get so low that you never rise above and move forward.

In order to be free, all you have to do is ask God for forgiveness, repent, and turn from your sin. When you do this, you receive the gifts of grace and mercy from God. When the enemy speaks lies that you are the same person you used to be and you'll never become this person God says you are, you must resist him. The enemy's lies drain you and weaken your resolve if you don't use your weapons.

Your weapon is your praise to God for making you free. Your weapon is the Word of God that lets you know who He says you are. Your weapon is the *truth*. For this reason, God is constantly reminding us throughout His Word of the truth: that we are His, loved, valuable, chosen, forgiven, and free. Don't let anyone tell you that you aren't who God says you are or that you'll never be who God wants you to be. Don't let Satan torment you with his nonsense. You are free. Speak life over yourself and walk in the freedom that Christ died for you to have.

Reflect and Pray

I reject the lie that I can't shake free from the bondage of my past. I embrace the truth that I'm free. I'm different now. I am not who I used to be, nor who others said I was.

Lord, thank You for my freedom. Thank You that sin no longer has me in its evil grasp and that I am free to leave my past behind me. Thank You for Your loving sacrifice that overpowered shame, guilt, and regret.

In Jesus' name, Amen.

I Am Redeemed

Has the LORD redeemed you? Then speak out!
Tell others he has redeemed you from your enemies.

Psalm 107:2, NLT

Redeemed means you have been *bought back*. The Bible says, "For the wages of sin is death; but the gift of God is eternal life through Jesus Christ our Lord" (Romans 6:23, KJV). This means that the worthy payment for our sin was death, but when Jesus died on the cross and rose again, He paid the price for our sin so we don't have to die or be enslaved to sin and we can live full, free lives in Him.

The enemy lures us to sin because he knows our failures make us run and hide from God. This is because when you make a mistake, Satan immediately sends condemnation to make you feel you can never get back in right standing with God. But when we quickly go to God and ask Him for forgiveness, God redeems us, taking away the burden, appearance, and residue of our wrongdoing. Our best response to this undeserved grace is to dedicate ourselves to repentance—deliberately turning from our sin and trying our very best not to live that way anymore.

Do you realize that long before you ever committed a sin, you had already been redeemed? God knew we would mess up. He did not create us to be perfect. He created us to lean and depend on Him, knowing that we could never enjoy a full life without Him. So God doesn't hold us to a standard of perfection, but He shows us in His Word how to lead a righteous life. A righteous person is not someone who's free of error, but who strives to please God in everything they do and to correct their course when they do not. Righteous does not mean you are perfect; it means you've been redeemed. In other words, you have been touched and changed by the power of God and made new once more.

When you've been redeemed, you can hold your head up high knowing that you are totally free not only from your sin, but also from its side effects. When Jesus hung on the cross, He gave you the right to be forgiven and freed by rescuing you from the consequences of sin. Because of Him, we can overcome and release the hold sin has over us and live to tell others about how far we've come.

Because you've been redeemed, you don't have to be afraid to share your testimony. This does not mean you have to tell every detail of what you've done or undergone. Some things aren't for everyone to hear or know. The Spirit of the Lord will lead you to share your testimony in a way that is uplifting, encouraging, and helpful to someone else who may be suffering the same things you have overcome. You are a living testimony that through the redeeming power of Jesus Christ, real change is possible.

In John 8:1-11, a woman caught in the act of adultery is brought before Jesus. Her accusers hoped Jesus would punish her, but Jesus did not condemn her nor punish her. He forgave her, extended grace, and redeemed her. "Go and sin no more," He told her, reminding us that guaranteed grace and forgiveness is by no means an excuse to keep on sinning. It is an opportunity to leave your sinful past behind you and begin a new life in God that is dedicated to loving and serving Him wholeheartedly.

Even though we are guilty, Jesus took the blame. You have a new lease of life. You get to walk in authority, knowing you are a living example of the power of God's grace. You no longer have any obligation to your past. You've been redeemed.

Reflect and Pray

I reject the lie that my past has the power to define or hold me. I embrace the truth that the Lord has redeemed me and changed my life completely.

Lord, thank You for rescuing me from the pain and anguish that came with my mistakes. Thank You for not leaving me where I fell, but instead placing my feet on solid ground once again. I wouldn't be here today if it weren't for You keeping me and rescuing me from the path of destruction I was on. Thank You for everything You've done.

In Jesus' name, Amen.

I Am Precious

For we are God's masterpiece. He has created us anew in Christ Jesus,
so we can do the good things he planned for us long ago.

Ephesians 2:10, NLT

Something that is precious is rare and irreplaceable, so it should be protected and handled with immense care. That is what God sees when He looks at you: someone who is special and essential to Him.

God wants you to be treated with the tender, loving care you deserve. This means you have the right to dismiss and reject anyone who mistreats you in word or deed. Don't let anyone hurt or abuse you physically, mentally, emotionally, or spiritually. Don't lower your standards and let another person pressure you into compromising your integrity. Don't hurt or abuse yourself by talking down to yourself—remember that death and life are in the power of your tongue (Proverbs 18:21).

Don't let the enemy make you think you don't matter to God, or that your past has cast a shadow over who you are to Him. You are just as important to God as the next person, and He doesn't want you to be misused, mistreated, trampled on, taken advantage of, or cast aside. He wants you to be respected and appreciated as the rare and precious jewel you are.

The company you keep is a reflection of how precious you know you are to God, so don't let others diminish the way you see yourself. Not just anyone should possess the privilege of occupying your presence and influencing your God-given identity. This doesn't mean you think you're better than anyone. It just means you refuse to give toxic people the ability to leave their impression on you.

You are extraordinary, exquisite, priceless, and magnificent. You are dearly loved by God. He took His time with you and He lovingly watches over you and your affairs on a daily basis. When we fail to guard ourselves from anything that seeks to tarnish the luster God gives us, we take for granted how precious we are to Him.

This is why the Word says to love the Lord with all your heart, soul, mind, and strength (Mark 12:30). Every part of you is precious and belongs to God. You are a one-of-a-kind creation that He absolutely adores. Only He knows how to fully love you the way you need and crave. When you prioritize your relationship with the One who made you, you will truly discover just how important it is to protect every part of yourself from being tainted by the pressures of this world.

Sometimes we think we know what we need, but God knows us better than we know ourselves. Ask Him to put people in your life who will love and appreciate you—people who are a good fit not only for where you are, but for where you're going. God knows the plans He has for you, and He knows how to place people in your life who value you and will help you grow in the things of God.

As your Shepherd, God tends to every part of you and everything that concerns you with the highest discretion. Trust Him completely by yielding your thoughts, plans, desires, opinions, wants, and needs to Him. He will handle you with care.

Reflect and Pray

I reject the lie that I am not a rare, prized, and precious creation of God. I embrace the truth that God carefully and lovingly made me to bring glory to His name.

Lord, thank You that I am precious to You. No matter what anyone else says or thinks about me, I am completely humbled and moved by the fact that I am of immense importance to You. Thank You for always treating me with lovingkindness and genuine care.

In Jesus' name, Amen.

I Am Protected

Those who go to God Most High for safety will be protected by the Almighty.
I will say to the LORD, "You are my place of safety and protection.
You are my God and I trust you."

Psalm 91:1-2, NCV

When you're protected, you are safe. You know that no pain, danger, difficulty, or distress has the power to destroy you. The weapon will form, but it will not prosper. In other words, trouble will come and it will affect you, but if you trust God, in the end you will still be standing tall. In fact, you will be better and stronger because of what you've been through.

The enemy wants you to feel exposed, unsafe, and afraid. He wants you to look at the world as one big, scary place full of tragedy. The truth is, unfortunate things happen to good people, and it isn't easy to watch or endure, but as long as you're in the will of God, you're covered. That calamity will not destroy you because God's plan is to prosper you. It is when we get out from underneath His shadow that we have every reason to fear tomorrow. God knows what's going to happen. He knows how the story ends, and no matter what happens, it ends in victory for you.

Sometimes we let fear get the best of us and cause us to believe that God won't take care of us. We entertain thoughts that say: *a loving God wouldn't allow such bad things to happen.* Don't let the enemy fill your mind with these lies. He wants you to doubt God's love for you. He wants you to lose your faith in God's power and ability to cover and keep you.

It's normal to want to understand why certain things happen, but we should guard our minds from losing faith in God's goodness. When your faith is unshakeable, you can remain standing despite enduring even the most trying, difficult, and fearsome storms and trials because of the power at work within you. God wants us to have faith in His ability to cover us. He won't leave you stranded, alone, and exposed to the enemy's attacks.

Jesus let us know that in this world we will have trouble, but we can take heart because He overcame the world (John 16:33). When you put your total trust in God, nothing the enemy tries to do will destroy you. He has no power and he certainly does not have the victory. There will be time when life's trials push your faith to the brink, but even then, you should lean on the Word of God which assures us: "We are hard pressed on every side, but not crushed; perplexed, but not in despair; persecuted, but not abandoned; struck down, but not destroyed" (2 Corinthians 4:8-9).

Anything God allows to happen in your life, He is working together for your good. God takes no delight in your pain, or seeing you try to defend yourself against the enemy on your own. When you try to protect yourself in your own strength, you're fighting a losing battle because this war is spiritual. Your fight is not against another person, it is against Satan, an enemy you cannot touch or see. For this reason, we must fight in the Spirit by praying, utilizing the armor God gives us, and depending on Him completely so we can overcome the enemy against all odds.

Be confident that your Father, your Creator, is sitting on the throne and He's watching. He does not sleep nor slumber. He sees what you cannot see, and He's protecting you from things you may not even realize you need protection from. He is guarding, covering, helping, and sustaining you, and He is not moved or surprised by the storm you see. He controls everything, so trust Him to act on your behalf.

Reflect and Pray

As a daughter of God, I reject the lie that the enemy has any power over me. I embrace the truth that God is on my side and protects me from harm and danger.

Lord, thank You for watching over and protecting me consistently, and never taking Your eyes or hands off my life. Thank You that I don't have to fear tomorrow or any negative thing coming against me because You are guarding and hiding me. I am confident that since You are in control of my life, You control every outcome.

In Jesus' name, Amen.

I Am Capable

We are not saying that we can do this work ourselves.
It is God who makes us able to do all that we do.

2 Corinthians 3:5, NCV

You can't do this. You've made too many mistakes. You don't have what it takes. Are you sure God told you? Just stop while you're ahead.

All these false, intimidating statements and thoughts come to make you question your ability to do what God told you to do. The enemy can't physically stop you from doing something. Instead, he attacks your mind and tries to get you to believe you don't possess the necessary qualities to complete the mission God has for you. His greatest fear is that you will rise above every challenge and become the woman God created and planned for you to be. He will send thought after thought designed to make you question yourself and doubt God's ability to work through you to bring His Word to pass.

Whatever God has called you to do, whatever season you're walking into, and whatever is required of you right now, know that *you can do this.* God wouldn't call you to do something without giving you all of the necessary qualities and requirements to see it through until the end, but you have to put your trust in Him. Sometimes you will feel like you just don't have it in you, or as though God should've chosen someone else. There will be times when the task seems harder than you have the capacity to conquer. Even when you start with all the excitement and confidence in the world, you can still get to the point where you feel like you're not the best or don't have what it takes to finish what you began.

You should know that even though you're the one doing the deed, God is the one who planted the seed. He would never raise you up and require you to do something without completely preparing you. When you don't feel capable, that's the moment you should lean even harder on God. You can't do this on your own but God can do it through you.

Don't let fear settle in your mind, making its home in the way you see yourself and the task at hand. Cast down those negative thoughts in their tracks and don't give them any room to take root in your mind. Yes, you can. Yes, you will.

God has given all of us gifts and tasks He is trusting us to accomplish, but it's going to take His strength, help, direction, and support. Without God, you can't do anything anyway. When you humble yourself and allow God to help, lead, and guide you, He will show you just how awesome and capable He is. He will exceed your expectations.

With God working through you, there is nothing you cannot do. You are unstoppable. You are a force to be reckoned with. You can and will succeed because God does not lose, so neither do you. Tell yourself every day that you are capable. You can do this. God is with you. He will not fail you.

Reflect and Pray

I reject the lie that I am not fully capable of success. I embrace the truth that I am capable because God is working through me and giving me the ability.

Lord, thank You for giving me what it takes to accomplish every task that is before me. Thank You for endowing me with the knowledge, power, and strength to see it through until the end. I will not give up because I know victory is mine.

In Jesus' name, Amen.

I Am Enough

Jesus has the power of God, by which he has given us everything we need to live and to serve God. We have these things because we know him. Jesus called us by his glory and goodness.

2 Peter 1:3, NCV

Do you ever feel like you aren't good enough? You do the best you can but those painful feelings of inadequacy still creep up. They tell you that you aren't a good enough Christian, sister, daughter, wife, mom, or friend. You pray every morning, yet the enemy still attacks you. You prepare for your day to go perfectly, but somehow, everything goes haywire. Despite all your efforts to accomplish your daily goals, something is always left undone.

Frustrating life events like these will leave you asking yourself, *will anything I do ever be enough?* Even when others praise your efforts, in your mind you're convinced you should have done or given more. You want to be perfect, to never make a mistake, and to excel in every area of your life.

You look at others and think, *they have it all figured out; nothing ever goes wrong for them.* You're convinced that your life pales in comparison to theirs. You wonder if and when your life will ever look the way you really want it to and hope for a change. As you focus on your insecurities, you magnify them over your capabilities, and you begin to feel your life is inadequate in every way.

You may not realize it, but by belittling your life, you are playing into the enemy's plan to keep you from seeing who and what God sees in you. God has blessed you to do some incredible things, and He wants to continue to shine through you. With Him working through you, you are more than enough.

It's good to aim for perfection but you can't do it all. Put your best foot forward and let God handle the rest. There will be days when you plan well for success but everything still won't go the way you hoped. Just because things go wrong doesn't mean that you aren't good enough. Sometimes things just happen. We can't control every outcome.

God not only wants you to know you are good enough, but also you *are* enough. End of story. Being enough means you don't need anything or anyone to satisfy or complete you because your wholeness is found in Christ alone. You don't need anyone to validate or confirm you. You aren't lacking in any area. This doesn't mean there isn't room for improvement, but your desire to change and grow doesn't negate the fact that your identity as a daughter of God is sufficient. You can be made whole in Him because He created you.

Don't believe the enemy's lies when he tells you someone else is better than you because it seems they've accomplished more than you have. Don't compare yourself to others and fail to see your own beauty and capabilities. Look in the mirror and see: you are enough.

Reflect and Pray

I reject the lie that I am inadequate, unworthy, or not good enough. I embrace the truth that God loves me—all of me—and His approval is all I need.

Lord, thank You that I don't have to search for anything or anyone to complete me or make me feel like I'm finally enough. I am already enough in You. Thank You for reminding me that I am whole and helping me continue to grow in You.

In Jesus' name, Amen.

I Am Not Alone

Have I not commanded you? Be strong and courageous. Do not be frightened, and do not be dismayed, for the LORD your God is with you wherever you go.

Joshua 1:9, ESV

No one wants to be alone. Sure, there are times when we want our own space or want some "alone time," but no one wants to be completely alone for the rest of their lives. If they do, it is likely because they have deeply rooted feelings of rejection. No matter how strong you are, isolation is problematic for anyone.

When you feel alone, you feel like you don't have anyone you can count on or turn to in times of need. Without someone trustworthy to confide in, you are more likely to hold in all your feelings, which is a building block for disaster.

God didn't create us to be lonely, solitary, isolated beings. He doesn't want us to live on this earth physically or emotionally alone. He created us for companionship—to give and receive love and affection, and to share in each other's triumphs and difficulties. The enemy wants you to feel like you can't depend on anyone, not even God. He wants you to think you're in this world all by yourself and that even the Lord is too preoccupied to love you through life's painful and discouraging moments. He will even try to make you believe your mistakes isolate you from God and others. The truth is, God never will abandon you, even if the entire world does. Loss can also make you feel alone and as though God has left you to fend for yourself, but no matter what happens, we should be sure that God is always with us. He will never leave you alone nor walk away from you, especially during times of trouble. We are never alone in our grief because God makes His presence even more real and directly accessible to us in those times.

Fight against those negative thoughts that cause you to believe you're all by yourself because you never are. Whatever situation you find yourself in, trust that God is in it with you and He will not forsake you.

When you feel alone, it's important to combat those thoughts with the truth: I am not alone. Begin praying and sharing your feelings with your Father. He wants to heal your heart, to lift you up out of the pit of despair and show you that His grace is sufficient for you. He won't leave you lonely, hurting, broken, or wounded. He won't cross to the other side of the road or close his eyes to your grief. He wants to shield you from the weight of life's hardest difficulties. He wants to shoulder the weight.

So the next time your situation makes you feel like you have to figure it out on your own and find a way through, remind yourself that God sees and understands you so much better than you can. Remind yourself you are not alone; He's with you. Always.

Reflect and Pray

I reject the lie that no one is with me or cares about what I'm going through. I embrace the truth that God cares and is always with me, so I am never alone.

Lord, thank You for standing with and for me, especially when I'm up against difficult trials that make me feel isolated and even afraid. I know there is never a time when I am alone because You are and always will be with me.

In Jesus' name, Amen.

I Am More Than a Conqueror

No, in all these things we are more than conquerors through him who loved us.

Romans 8:37, ESV

Defeat can be hard to overcome, especially because you're up against a lot. Every day you are faced with any number of obstacles concerning your family, job, self-esteem, mindset, and unforeseen circumstances that require urgent or immediate action. Life is hard, but it's far harder if you aren't completely depending on God.

Jesus said, "The thief comes only to steal and kill and destroy. I came that they may have life and have it abundantly" (John 10:10, ESV). When Satan attacks, his intent is to defeat you any way possible. He doesn't want you to succeed and he is afraid that you will become a force to be reckoned with in the kingdom of God. As a child of God, you are a threat to Satan's plan to wreak havoc in this world. As long as you're living for God, he will constantly fight against you.

Since you know that Satan is already defeated, and God has all power, this shouldn't frighten you. In fact, you should be all the more encouraged to know that you are a conqueror. So there's nothing the enemy can do to take you out. A conqueror is someone who overcomes any obstacle that comes their way. Every battle won't be an easy win, but through confidence and faith in God, you will be successful despite difficulty.

A conqueror doesn't give up easily. They don't back down without a fight and they certainly never surrender. When you're faced with opposition beyond what you expected or understand, don't give up on yourself and don't give up on God. His power shows up best when you are at your weakest. He wants you to allow His power to win this battle.

When David fought Goliath, he knew he was well able to conquer him— not because David was a mighty and powerful soldier, but because he had seen God show up for him before. He knew that God would never fail or leave him. David was also confident in himself because he knew God's anointing and favor was on his life and that God had given him the tools he needed to conquer this giant. Sometimes we have confidence in God but we lack confidence in ourselves. You should be sure that if God is for you, He's more than the world that is against you.

The enemy wants you to think this battle is too big for you and for God. He wants you to give up before it even begins because he knows something he doesn't want you to know: with God on your side, you already won. Don't let your adversary get in your ear and psych you out of obtaining the victory.

This will not break you and it will not overtake you. You are a warrior, a soldier, and a mighty conqueror in the kingdom of God. This battle is the Lord's: He's just using you as His vessel. In the end, you will still be standing strong because God does not lose.

Reflect and Pray

I reject the lie that I am not more than able to conquer this giant, this mountain, this struggle, or this obstacle. I embrace the truth that my God is more than able to give me the strength and power to overcome any difficulty I face.

Lord, thank You for making me more than a conqueror and giving me the victory in the battle I'm facing now. I know that with You on my side, I can't lose, so I give You all the glory, honor, and praise for the win.

In Jesus' name, Amen.

I Am Fearfully and Wonderfully Made

*I praise you, for I am fearfully and wonderfully made. Wonderful are your works;
my soul knows it very well.*

Psalm 139:14, ESV

You have probably heard these words many times, but have you ever considered what it really means to be fearfully and wonderfully made?

To be fearfully made means God took His time with you to make sure every little detail about you was the epitome of perfection. You are complex, multi-faceted, and multi-dimensional. You are beautiful. You are creative. You are incredible. You have the endless capacity to do amazing things. God was not rushing when He made you and He didn't cut any corners. You are not lacking in any way. You are the apple of God's eye—His highest creation—and He is so proud of you.

To be wonderfully made means God did His job exceedingly well. You are not a mistake. You are not a failure. You are not a problem or inconvenience. You're everything God wants you to be, His prized possession. So it's time for you to start believing you are everything and more to Him.

We do not get to determine our family background, where we grow up, what we will look like, how we will be raised, what will happen to us, or what struggles we will have to overcome. Remember, long before you were even a thought in your parents' minds, God had an intricate and incredible plan for your life. He designed a specific purpose that He only wants you to fill. He wants you to make your mark on this world by being who He created you to be.

You have unique features, characteristics, gifts, and talents that God specifically formulated to fit into His kingdom like a missing puzzle piece. This is why Satan wants you to think you're not all that special compared to others. If he can get you to believe the lies that you don't fit, you don't matter, you aren't important, or you aren't necessary, then you will miss out on all of the great and mighty things God has planned for your life.

God didn't create you to lead an average or mediocre life. He doesn't want you to look back in 20, 40, or 60 years and wish you had done more, lived more, or reached for more. He wants you to know that He patiently and carefully crafted you to live an abundant life full of blessing, beauty, and wonder.

And the best part is, God's not finished with you yet! Isn't that amazing? The same God who made you *still* isn't done with you. Philippians 1:6 (ESV) says: "And I am sure of this, that he who began a good work in you will bring it to completion at the day of Jesus Christ." You are a brilliant, fascinating, and beautiful work of art, and God wants to continue to advance you.

When God looks at you, He has to take a step back and say, "Wow, I outdid myself!" That's how remarkable you are to Him. Every ounce of you has purpose and God's hands are on your life. You should be ever-growing, ever-changing, and ever-improving as His daughter.

Reflect and Pray

I reject the lie that I'm "just average" or "not that special." I embrace the truth that an incredible God made an incredible me to fulfill an incredible purpose in this world.

Lord, thank You for taking your time with me and creating me with a purpose. Thank You for all of my unique qualities and characteristics that make me who I am in You. Please help me use the gifts and talents You've given me for Your glory.

In Jesus' name, Amen.

WHATEVER IS NOBLE

Don't just act noble. Be noble.

The word "noble" speaks to a person's character. Noble means honorable, honest, worthy of respect, and uncorrupted. If we think on what it means to be noble, we are essentially thinking on what it means to be more like Christ, who exemplified nobility in everything He did. He thought highly of Himself and others, and refused to behave in a manner that wasn't in accordance with His flawless character, despite being fully human. Just like you and me, there were times He was tempted to be unkind, unfriendly, or to act in fear, but He decided to be kind. He decided to be friendly. He decided to be brave.

Every day you wake up, you get to decide who and how you're going to be. Are you going to be rude, conniving, dishonest, and mean? Or are you going to be noble? A noble person thinks highly of herself and others. She does not just *act* loving, honest, loyal, or understanding when it is easy or convenient. She *is* all of these things, regardless of circumstance. When you make the conscious decision to stop being spiteful, disrespectful, reckless, petty, or prideful, and begin to consistently imitate the attitude and behavior of Christ—who was respectful, wise, and humble—these admirable qualities will naturally become part of who you are.

God is not calling us to merely *act* noble, but to *be* noble. Yes, it is easier said than done, but in order to become noble like Christ, we have to think higher about ourselves and others. If we want to reflect the characteristics of God, we have to stop giving in to the fleshly inclination that naturally goes against anything that is honest and good in God's eyes. Changing your behavior will not happen overnight, nor will it come without a fight, but it's worth it to be that much closer to who God is calling you to be.

In this section, we will explore 15 noble characteristics God wants us to adopt in exchange for their opposites. As you progress through this section, remember that you are capable of change and improvement. Don't try to "fake it until you make it." As you take it one day at a time, one noble characteristic at a time, and give God your best effort towards making real change, God will honor your effort and help you become more like Him.

Regardless of who I am or have been, I can and want to be noble like Christ. I will think highly of myself and others, in order to make noble decisions and become a noble daughter of God.

Be Loving

Don't just pretend to love others. Really love them. Hate what is wrong. Hold tightly to what is good. Love each other with genuine affection, and take delight in honoring each other.

Romans 12:9-10, NLT

Since God is love, having a relationship with Him requires and encourages us to be loving like He is. God loves always, not just when His affection is reciprocated. If we really want to be like Christ, we have to follow His example and learn to love others unconditionally. Everywhere He went, Jesus showed love because love is a fundamental characteristic of God.

God knows when you really love someone. He knows your heart and can recognize when you're just going through the motions so you can say that you "showed love." True love is deeper than a feeling; it's even more than a simple action. True love comes from a spiritual connection with God because He *is* love. Without God working in and through us, we will only experience a *form* of love. We will only be able to scratch the surface. If we truly want to be loving, we must draw closer to God and allow Him to love *through* us.

There may be people in your life who you feel are hard to love for many different, complicated reasons. No matter what someone does to you or how trying they can be at times, the closer you draw to God, the more He will fill your heart with the desire and ability to love people truthfully and completely. 1 Peter 4:8 says, "Above all, love each other deeply, because love covers over a multitude of sins" (NIV). When you love deeply, you can love beyond every hurt, rejection, and offense that has happened to you. Regardless of circumstance, you'll be able to forgive and move forward.

God doesn't want us to put up a fake front, but to genuinely love people, just like He does. God's love isn't conditional—we've hurt, offended, and disappointed God countless times yet He still loves us. Every day God sets the example of the love He wants us to follow. So aim to love others the way you want to be loved: in a way that is kind, considerate, and real. To be loving, you have to be willing to put others before yourself, and to honor them in every way.

Hatred is not the opposite of love; it is the *absence* of it. Many of us think we're doing good as long as we don't have hatred in our hearts. Love has two real enemies: indifference, and fear. Indifference expressed is a blatant disregard for another person's feelings and overall well-being: which is not loving at all. Showing others that you don't care one way or another about their feelings or value your relationship with them is not at all Christlike and shows a lack of closeness with Him. Fear, on the other hand, is often a result of hurt and rejection, that prevents you from wanting to be vulnerable and open yourself up to love and be loved by others.

If you really want to be loving, prioritize your relationship with God. He is the epitome of love and everything He says and does is in love. The closer you get to Him, the more loving you will become because it is a natural byproduct of spending time in His presence. You are capable of loving more, but it requires thoughtfulness, intention, and change.

Reflect and Pray

No longer will I be indifferent towards or fearful of expressing true love. Instead, I will be loving.

Lord, thank You for showing me the true definition of love that You desire for me to follow. Thank You for helping me not to be unloving, hateful, indifferent, or afraid. Thank You for helping me love the way that You do.

In Jesus' name, Amen.

Be Friendly

Nothing should be done because of pride or thinking about yourself.
Think of other people as more important than yourself.

Philippians 2:3, NLV

"Friend" is a term that people use loosely, but a real friend is not easy to find. Many people don't know how to be a friend while others don't know how to *have* a friend—how to appreciate and reciprocate the loving companionship they have received.

A real friend communicates with you and is honest—they don't just tell you what you want to hear. A real friend invests in you; they care for you, are concerned about you, and pray for you. They are loyal and trustworthy despite disagreements. They do not abandon you when trouble arises but will remain consistently supportive. A real friend will do anything they can to help you. They genuinely and unconditionally love you, want God's best for you, and never give up on you. True friendship is a *commitment*, and commitments are meant to be binding, not easily broken.

Sometimes you can be a friend to someone who is not a friend (or as good a friend) to you. Proverbs 18:24 says, "A man who has friends must *himself* be friendly..." (NLV). Friendly means: kind, considerate, accessible, affectionate, and helpful. Jesus was referred to as a "friend of sinners" in the Bible (Luke 17:34) because He did not let a person's mistakes stop Him from loving them and being friendly. He didn't let others negatively influence Him, but *He* influenced *them* by showing grace and mercy, loving them without judgment, and inviting them into relationship with Him.

No one wants to be in a one-sided friendship, but sometimes God may bless you to be a friend to someone who needs you more than you need them. Let God show you who He wants you to be a friend to. You may be the encouragement they desperately need to access a better life in Christ. It's important to recognize when God wants to use you in this way, and to put your own needs aside in the interest of your friend's well-being.

Don't be taken advantage of; seek God to show you what to do and say in every situation. The best thing you can do for your friend is pray for them. You won't always be able to help improve their situation and you certainly cannot change anyone, but with God, all things are possible, and your earnest prayers have great power to yield prosperous results.

A wonderful example of this is in Mark 2:1-12, where a paralyzed man's four friends literally go above and beyond to help him get to Jesus. There were crowds of people in the house hoping to see Jesus, so the men couldn't get through the front door. But they were so determined to see their friend made whole that they dug a hole through the clay roof of the house and lowered the sick man on his stretcher down to Jesus. Jesus then forgave the man's sins based upon the faith of his four friends, *and* heals him! If it weren't for this man's friends, he wouldn't have been made whole: physically healed and spiritually redeemed. That is the power of true friendship.

Reflect and Pray

No longer will I be an unfaithful, unconcerned, or selfish "friend." I will be a real friend who acts with the love of Christ.

Lord, thank You for showing me that my friendship is important and powerful. Please help me to be a real friend towards those You put in my life for me to show Your love. Help me to refrain from only loving those who love me in return.

In Jesus' name, Amen.

Be Loyal

If you love someone, you will be loyal to him no matter what the cost.
You will always believe in him, always expect the best of him,
and always stand your ground in defending him.

1 Corinthians 13:7, TLB

A loyal friend is a rare and precious gift. When God blesses you with a true and loyal friend, be sure to cherish and appreciate this person because it is an honor and a privilege to have them in your life. A loyal friend will love and support you no matter what. They are faithful, reliable, and unwavering in their love for you. They are concerned about you and willing to go the distance to express their devotion to you. They are trustworthy and you can count on them to do what they said they were going to do. Even when you're not around, they will not betray you, but will defend you. They strengthen, support, encourage, and help you as much as they can.

Proverbs 20:6 says, "Many will tell you they're your loyal friends, but who can find one who is truly trustworthy?" (TPT). We all want trustworthy friends whose love and dedication to us is unquestionable, but it's not enough to have or desire loyal friends. You have to prove to your friends that you, too, are the real deal. You have to embody the traits and characteristics that you hope to have in your friend, showing them that they can count on you. Are you worthy of the trust you expect from that person? Are you committed to them, no matter the cost?

It's easy to be loyal when the person hasn't hurt or offended you, but could you be loyal to someone who betrayed you? Sometimes, when friends fall out with each other, they are quick to discredit the entire relationship. They spitefully tell all of their friend's business because they are hurt and want to get back at them. Even when a person lets us down, God wants us to still be loyal to them the way He is to us. He doesn't want us to be messy, petty, or vindictive, but to take the high road and remain loyal. Friends will come and go, but your decision to be loyal should remain consistent regardless of others' actions. This is about you and God, so you should aim to behave in a way that is pleasing to Him—and He doesn't turn His back on us when we let Him down.

Maybe you've been let down by someone you considered a friend. In Matthew 26, Judas, one of Jesus' twelve handpicked disciples, betrays Jesus to the chief priests who were looking for a way to capture and kill Jesus. Judas brings them directly to Jesus, and Judas embraces Jesus "in friendly fashion," pretending he has done no wrong. (Matthew 26:49, TLB). Even though Jesus knows Judas has betrayed Him, He says to Judas, "My friend, go ahead and do what you have come for" (v. 50). Despite Judas' betrayal, Jesus still calls him "friend." Jesus has every right to be upset and indignant, but instead, He is kind and merciful. He doesn't turn his back on Judas but loves him and remains loyal to him, even though Judas set Jesus up to die. Now *that's* loyalty.

Loyalty is not letting others walk all over you, it's choosing to maintain your good character despite temptation, or the negligent, malicious, and selfish acts of others. When you learn how to be loyal to others the way God is to you and keep your ultimate trust in Him and not in human beings, He will bless you with friends who will not let you down.

Reflect and Pray

No longer will I be disloyal, untrustworthy, or unreliable. I will show myself friendly and be loyal.

Lord, thank You for showing me in Your Word the importance of being loyal. Thank You for helping me commit to being a loyal friend to others. Even if I am hurt or offended, help me to honor You in my response.

In Jesus' name, Amen.

Be Kind

Be kind to one another, tenderhearted, forgiving one another,
as God in Christ forgave you.

Ephesians 4:32, ESV

Kindness is a quality that cannot be forced or feigned. The difference between being "nice" and being kind can be summarized in a single word: authenticity. Nice is a surface description that does not have to stem from the heart. It is *nice* to smile at someone. It is *kind* to take a genuine interest in how they are doing today. Kindness is all about generosity towards and consideration for others, which means you can't be kind *and* selfish. To be kind, you have to genuinely love others and be willing to sacrifice your own resources in order to show them that you care.

Kindness brews continually from a heart that is steeped in the love and compassion of Christ, which propels you to extend kindness whenever and however you can. Kindness, like mercy, is unconcerned with merit. God daily shows us kindness, not so that we will become hoarders, but so we'll pay it forward and show kindness to everyone we encounter. God wants kindness to become our natural reaction even when people are rude or indifferent. Receiving the kindness of God and purposing ourselves to be kind in spite of how we are treated will only cause God to pour His favor out on us all the more.

Kindness is a fruit of the Spirit—a product of God's presence dwelling inside you, and because God is love, being kind to someone is an act of love. It pleases God when we put others before ourselves and go out of our way to help them without needing or expecting reciprocity. It's nice when our kindness is returned, and God will bless you with relationships where that is the norm but be careful not to create transactional relationships by only doing things for others because you anticipate they will return the favor down the line. Those kinds of relationships are built on expectation, not love. When your expectations aren't met, you likely won't jump at the opportunity to do something kind for the person again, which isn't the most Christlike approach to relationships. Work to create friendships where you are bonded by love, not deeds.

Proverbs 11:17 says, "Your kindness will reward you, but your cruelty will destroy you" (NLT). Sometimes the way others have treated us throughout our lives makes us reluctant to be kind because it hurts when that kindness is abused or unappreciated. Don't let those negative experiences harden you to the point where you approach life with closed fists, never wanting to give to others because you refuse to be hurt or taken advantage of again. Allow God to heal your heart from the disappointment those situations caused. Open your hands to both pour out and receive kindness once again.

Reflect and Pray

No longer will I let yesterday's hurt keep me from showing kindness to my neighbor. From this day forward, I'm determined to be kind, generous, and considerate.

Lord, thank You that You are kind and that through Your Spirit, You are enabling me to bear this attribute. Help me to let go of anything hindering me from extending the same kindness You show me daily to others.

In Jesus' name, Amen.

Be Compassionate

When he saw the crowds, he had compassion for them, because they were harassed and helpless, like sheep without a shepherd. Then he said to his disciples, 'The harvest is plentiful, but the laborers are few.'

Matthew 9:36-37, ESV

Compassion is a strong feeling of care, sympathy, concern, and pity for the needs of others that stirs the desire to help them in some way. Compassion is the very nature of God, who loves us so much that He looks *beyond* our faults and sees our needs. Compassion is simply *love in action*. You don't have to know a person to show compassion. The Good Samaritan showed compassion to a complete stranger who did not share the same background as him. Compassion should be readily extended to anyone and everyone to whom God wants you to show His love.

Being compassionate doesn't mean you will agree with everything a person does. In spite of the things we do wrong, God is still full of compassion for us. You won't always like how people treat you, but when you are compassionate, you become able to look past their indiscretions and recognize they need love.

There will be people God puts in your path for you to show compassion. Jesus said the poor and needy will be with us always (Matthew 26:11), and God is counting on us to make a difference in their lives, but He wants us to have the right heart posture. Anyone can feed or clothe people, but not just anyone can show them compassion. The reason why people loved and clung to Jesus so much wasn't just because of what He could do for them, but because He showed them compassion. Jesus didn't just listen to them but He expressed sincere interest in their concerns *and* helped them.

In Matthew 14, John the Baptist is beheaded and buried, and Jesus is much grieved because John was a close friend of His. Jesus goes by boat to a deserted place to be alone, but the people are eager to be around Him and follow Him. It wouldn't have been selfish for Jesus to take some time for Himself, but He is so moved with compassion for them that not only does He heal their sick, but He miraculously feeds them—well over 5,000 people—using five loaves of bread and two fish. In one of His most difficult times, Jesus puts Himself aside for the needs of others, going out of His way to love and help them.

Jesus shows us that true compassion is putting your own needs, desires, and feelings aside in order to tend to someone else in their time of need. The compassion Jesus showed required that He depend on the strength of the Lord. You will go through incredibly difficult circumstances in life that will cause you to want to focus on what you're going through. Even then, God still wants to use you to be compassionate because it will point others toward Him. Second Corinthians 1:4 says that God "comforts us every time we have trouble, so when others have trouble, we can comfort them with the same comfort God gives us" (NCV). Even when your world is falling apart, if you lean into God and let Him be your strength, you will still be able to smile, give someone a hug, lend a helping hand, or share an encouraging word.

Reflect and Pray

No longer will I look only to my own needs, but I will be compassionate toward the needs of others.

Lord, thank You for how You've shown me such abundant compassion, looking past my faults and comforting me when I needed it the most. Please help me to show this same Christlike love towards others in their time of need.

In Jesus' name, Amen.

Be Patient

But let patience have its perfect work, that you may be perfect
and complete, lacking nothing.

James 1:4, NKJV

Good things come to those who wait. All in good time. Haste makes waste. One step at a
time. Patience is a virtue.

When you're in a season of waiting, these clichés may bring little to no comfort, but they are all true. Even though we're impatient sometimes, God is not. Unlike us, He is completely unlimited by time. He knows exactly when He wants things to happen in our lives and why. He wants us to learn how to be patient in His will while expecting for Him to do great and mighty things in our lives.

Learning how to patiently wait for God to act yields the ability to be patient with others. You may be waiting for someone you love to change or improve in a certain area. Pray for them and encourage them to strive for better. Change does not happen overnight, but don't give up on them. It takes time and patience to see the results you are expecting, but all things are possible with God.

When you patiently wait on God, it shows that you trust Him and His timing. You're willing to wait for Him to do what He said without jumping to conclusions and moving ahead of time. During this time of waiting the enemy will try his best to invade your thoughts and get you to become discouraged, angry, resentful, or anxious that it won't happen. Impatience will cause you to try to "help God out," prolonging the process and delaying your blessing because you haven't learned the lessons God wants you to gain in your waiting. Trust that whatever God has for you will happen in His timing. It doesn't matter how long it takes, it's on the way.

In Genesis 12:2, Abraham (then Abram) is 75 years old when God promises him that he will become the father of a great nation. In Genesis 15:4, God tells Abraham that he will have a son. But ten years later, he and his wife Sarah (then Sarai) still have no children. Sarah then suggests Abraham sleep with her servant Hagar so they can have a son through her. Abraham agrees, and Hagar has a son named Ishmael. For the next 13 years, Abraham convinces himself that Ishmael is the son God promised him until God once again promises Abraham that he will have a son, this time stating specifically that it will happen through Sarah. At 90 years old, Sarah gives birth to Isaac 25 years after God originally promised that Abraham would become the father of a great nation.

God always delivers on His promises and He is worth waiting for. God doesn't need your help to accomplish His will, He just needs your obedience. Great blessings take time, so don't rush the process. This time of waiting is causing you to develop and mature spiritually, mentally, emotionally, physically, and financially. God wants you to be ready in every area of your life for what He's getting ready to do for you. Don't be hasty. Don't be impatient. Persevere in your faith and continually draw closer to God. Give Him praise for what He promised you. His blessings will amaze you and exceed even your wildest expectations.

Reflect and Pray

No longer will I wait in anger or resentment. I will be patient with God and others.

Lord, thank You for what You've promised to do in my life. I believe that You will do exactly what You said You will do and I'm willing to wait for it to come to pass. Thank You for helping me continue to do Your will as I look with expectancy for Your promises to be fulfilled in my life.

In Jesus' name, Amen.

Be Respectful

Don't forget to show hospitality to strangers, for some who have done this have entertained angels without realizing it!

Hebrews 13:2, NLT

Respect will take you a long way in life. When you treat people with high regard and are considerate of how your words and actions make them feel, you win favor with them and more important, with God. When you are disrespectful, unkind, and unsympathetic, you forfeit divine opportunities to share the love of Jesus and be blessed by God for honoring others.

Most children are taught the "Golden Rule," to treat others how you want to be treated. Jesus puts it this way: "Do to others whatever you would like them to do to you" (Matthew 7:12, NLT). But as adults our behavior often reflects a different rule: "do to others whatever they do to you," or "do to others whatever you believe they deserve." But treating people how you feel like treating them simply isn't the Christ way, so you have to push yourself to be respectful regardless of how you feel. And just because someone disrespects you does not give you the right to do the same to them. God wants us to take the high road and learn to show His love to our enemies—the ones who actually need it the most.

Respect is not just about what you say, but *how* you say it—your tone—so think carefully about your words before you speak them and do so with love and kindness. Also, your disposition can have an entire conversation with someone without you even opening your mouth. No one likes to be looked down on, mistreated, or judged, which are all forms of disrespect that God despises.

Respect is an attitude and a courtesy that should be shown across the board, but that doesn't mean you don't have the right to stand your ground and defend yourself when necessary. Even when others discredit or offend you, you can respectfully correct them and walk away if the situation escalates beyond your ability to control your response. God is eager to defend us when we leave vengeance in His hands: "'Do not take revenge, my dear friends, but leave room for God's wrath, for it is written: "It is mine to avenge; I will repay,' says the Lord" (Romans 12:19, NIV).

The world would be a better place if we all respected each other's opinions and right to make our own decisions. You won't agree with everyone, but you should always respect others in a loving way that allows for them to see Christ in you. Always remember that it's not about you, but the glory of God, so keep yourself in a position where He can use you.

Showing respect is the Godly way of handling any situation. Sometimes the enemy will use people to try to get a rise out of you because you're a Christian. Remember that everywhere you go, you are a representation of God, so it's important to keep a right attitude. You never know who God will use to bless you, and you can easily miss out on blessings God has for you by being rude or disrespectful when that person may be the vessel God was going to use.

Reflect and Pray

No longer will I be impolite towards others. I will honor God by respecting everyone.

Lord, thank You for showing me that respecting others is the Godly way of showing love. Please help me to respect everyone, whether or not I agree with them, and in spite of how a person makes me feel.

In Jesus' name, Amen.

Be Humble

Therefore humble yourselves under the mighty hand of God,
that He may exalt you in due time.

1 Peter 5:6, NKJV

God has an important calling on your life and He has chosen you to fulfill a great purpose for His kingdom, but it requires you to stay humble. The higher you go in God the more responsibility He gives you and the more blessings He bestows on you as you aim to do what pleases Him. When you're humble and committed to following God's will for your life, Him becomes more eager to bless you because He knows you're relying on Him, and God loves taking care of His children. When you don't humble yourself, you open the door for pride, which hinders God's ability to use and bless you.

In the Bible, pride is the belief that you are self-sufficient and don't need God. Pride was the original sin that resulted in Lucifer's (Satan's) fall from grace. As a mighty and anointed angel whose name meant "Son of the morning," Lucifer had the high honor of guarding the very throne of God. Over time, he became so impressed with the beauty, power, splendor, and intelligence God had blessed him with that he wanted to be greater than God, so God banished Lucifer from Heaven. Now, knowing that he is already defeated, Satan plots to destroy as many people as possible by spreading the same darkness that hardened his heart against God.

It is so important to praise and worship God daily, centering your focus on your Creator, and telling Him how much He means to you. A humble person gladly worships God, and doesn't let success, money, attention, or fame change who they are. Remember that your identity is found in Christ, not people or things. God will bless you even more when you remain humble despite success because He knows you love Him for who He is *to* you, not just what He does *for* you.

Joseph's story is one of the greatest examples of humility in the Bible. Joseph is only 17 when his brothers sell him into slavery because they are jealous that their father, Jacob, loves Joseph more than the rest of them, and because Joseph has divinely prophetic dreams. Potiphar, one of Pharaoh's officers, purchases Joseph. The Lord then blesses Joseph to excel while working for Potiphar, and he becomes Potiphar's personal attendant until Potiphar's wife falsely accuses Joseph of raping her, and he is forced to spend years in prison. But God vindicates him when Joseph successfully interprets Pharaoh's dreams, and Pharaoh makes Joseph his second in command in all of Egypt—a position that comes with riches, power, and renown. Yet despite all the success Joseph has acquired, he doesn't flaunt his assets when he is finally reunited with his brothers. Joseph knows he wouldn't have his title if it weren't for the favor of God on his life, so he forgives and blesses his brothers, taking care of them and their children.

The way to stay humble is to always recognize God as your life source. God is the source of your success, talents, gifts, joy, peace, strength, protection, and everything else you need. When you lose sight of God and start to believe that you are the source, you cut yourself off from the favor of God, which will get you farther than anything you can make happen for yourself. Remember that He is your Provider, so humble yourself and let Him lift you up.

Reflect and Pray

I will not let anything or anyone change who I am. I will stay humble, knowing that God is my source.

Lord, thank You for everything You have blessed me with and allowed me to do. I know that I am and could do nothing without You so I will remain humble so that You will continue to use me. Thank You for every blessing You bestow upon me as a result of obeying You.

In Jesus' name, Amen.

Be Faithful

Only fear the LORD *and serve him faithfully with all your heart.*
For consider what great things he has done for you.

1 Samuel 12:24, ESV

We use the word "faithful" when describing God because His consistency assures us that we can trust Him. He always does what He says He will. God is faithful to love, faithful to forgive, and faithful to perform. Every word He speaks is true, so we can stand firm on His promises.

God's desire is that we strive to be faithful like Him. When you are faithful, you are dedicated to God's will and you consistently love and serve Him. No matter what obstacles come your way, you are constant and unwavering in your faith. You're committed to God and refuse to give up on Him. A faithful servant of God will encounter challenges but is confident that God will protect and provide for them.

Don't let anything cause you to take your eyes off of what God has you stewarding right now. He will bless you with much more if you show Him that you can be faithful with this level of responsibility. God will not forsake you but He will help you continue to do what pleases Him the most. God's eyes shine on His faithful ones because He needs dependable servants that He can count on to carry out His purpose in this world.

One of the greatest Biblical examples of faithfulness is David. God anointed David as king of Israel while he was still a shepherd boy and after being anointed, David went right back to tending his father's sheep. He didn't let his excitement about becoming king one day distract him from remaining faithful to the task at hand, and years later, he indeed became king over all of Israel.

Many of the things that God wants to do in your life will depend on you remaining faithful to what He wants you to do right now. Prove to God that even though you're expecting Him to great and mighty things in your life, you will not forsake giving your best now as you patiently wait for Him to deliver on what He said. Be faithful in your efforts to please God in everything you do and He will bless you tremendously. Be faithful over your household. Be faithful over your money. Be faithful in serving others. Be faithful in prayer. Be faithful in this season. The enemy will try his best to discourage and distract you from staying the course because He knows that God's blessings overtake those who are faithful despite trials or temptations to give up.

Make it your goal to mirror God's faithfulness. He is faithful in keeping His promises to us, so our right response is to be faithful in keeping our promises to Him by working daily to please Him in everything we do. When you show God that you are faithful to His will, He will eagerly bless you for your actions and consistency.

Reflect and Pray

No longer will I lose sight of what God wants me to do. I will remain faithful to His will for my life and live in His purpose.

Lord, thank You for the promise you've given me and for Your incredible calling on my life. Please help me to remain faithful and committed to Your will every day just like You are always faithful to me. Thank You for keeping Your Word and for giving me something great to look forward to.

In Jesus' name, Amen.

Be Confident

For the LORD *will be your confidence and will keep your foot from being caught.*

Proverbs 3:26, ESV

Confidence is being sure of yourself because of the God you serve. When you're confident, you are certain that you're capable of doing what God called you to do—not by any goodness of your own, but because you know God is helping you and supplying you with everything necessary to get the job done. When Satan can't stop you from doing what God told you to do, he will always attack your confidence, hoping you'll give up out of fear that you don't have what it takes to fulfill your God-given mission.

Oftentimes, it's easier to have confidence in God than in ourselves. God's ability is sure and proven, but we sometimes let the enemy talk us out of doing what God wants us to do because we aren't sure we will be successful. You have to know without a shadow of a doubt that if God called you to do something, He has already made you more than able to see it through. It doesn't matter what level of knowledge, skill, or talent you feel you possess; God knows you're capable because He's living inside of you and He does not fail.

Whatever God has placed in your heart, don't be afraid to see it through! You must have the mindset that you are chosen and that you will win. Do not begin with the expectation of failure. Encourage yourself and recognize that God wouldn't call you to do something He hadn't already equipped you to successfully accomplish. God knows everything about you—your past, your failures, and your shortcomings., He chose you anyway. So why do we let the enemy use those things against us and talk us out of pursuing God's will for our lives? He knows he can't make you do anything, so he taunts you with thoughts of possible failure. You're better than that so don't let Satan overwhelm your mind with anxious, frightening thoughts that only impede your progress and delay the victory God has already promised you.

When God appeared to Moses and commanded him to lead the children of Israel out of captivity in Egypt, Moses lacked confidence in himself and gave God every excuse in the book. He didn't feel qualified, he didn't believe he was good enough or wise enough, he feared speaking in public, and he didn't think people would listen to him. With every excuse, God reassured Moses that He was with him and was everything he needed. Moses found confidence in himself through the realization that God had great confidence in him and was counting on him.

So what if someone else has done something similar to what God told you to do? Evidently you have something fresh and unique to add to the space, or God wouldn't have given it to you. Regardless how many people are doing something, there is still room for you. You don't have to know it all or have everything figured out. God knows what He placed inside of you and He just needs for you to confidently pursue His will. You are not alone—God will help you in every way.

Reflect and Pray

No longer will I feel like I'm not qualified or unable to conquer the task before me. I will be confident in God.

Lord, thank You for choosing me to fulfill this mission and giving me success. I will be confident in You and in myself, knowing that You never fail so victory is mine.

In Jesus' name, Amen.

Be Courageous

Don't be afraid, for I am with you. Don't be discouraged, for I am your God.
I will strengthen you and help you. I will hold you up
with my victorious right hand.

Isaiah 41:10, NLT

Doing great things for God requires great courage. You're going to have to confront every fear that attempts to stand between you and what God has for you. No, it will not be easy.

Courage is bravery in the face of fear. Courage is staying the course even though opposition is on the path. Courage is boldly declaring the Word of God over your life even when it looks like victory is not sure. Courage enables you to do more than you ever thought you could do.

Any time you set out to do something for God, the enemy wages war against you and he does not fight fair. It takes courage to stand up against your adversary but you have all of heaven backing you up. Besides, the devil is already defeated and he has no power over you. God's will for your life is worth the fight. Satan knows God has amazing things in store for you and he hates to see you blessed, happy, and successful. Every lie, threat, and attack by the enemy will fall flat when you courageously stand on the Word of God.

It took great courage for Joshua to succeed Moses as the leader of the Israelites when Moses died. Just before his death, Moses lays his hands on Joshua, who is then filled with the spirit of wisdom, and Joshua immediately becomes the next leader. Joshua was Moses' assistant, so losing Moses is devastating, but after thirty days of mourning, he has to move forward with God's plan. Realizing that he must now guide the people into Canaan, the Promised Land, feels like an insurmountable task to Joshua until God reassures him: "'Have I not commanded you? Be strong and courageous. Do not be frightened, and do not be dismayed, for the LORD your God is with you wherever you go'" (Joshua 1:9, ESV). Joshua obeys God and God grants him success over all his enemies.

God knows that the task you're up against is daunting, but the only way to overcome your fear of failure is to face it. When you decide to move forward with the plan God has given you, despite how difficult or impossible it appears, God gives you the strength to make it over every hurdle. Show God that you're willing to step up to the plate and He will use you once again to prove that nothing is impossible with Him.

Courage shows you have faith in God because you're believing that His promises are true. When you set out to fulfill a mission for God, don't let the obstacles thwart you. Lean back on what God promised you and remember that God does not lie and He does not lose. He will not allow you to be defeated by your enemy. Anything that happens to you in the will of God is because He allowed it, so it will work together for your good. Opposition will come, but overcoming adversity makes the ultimate victory so much sweeter.

Reflect and Pray

No longer will I give up in the face of fear. I will courageously depend on God to defend me and grant me victory.

Lord, thank You for giving me the strength I need to overcome every mountain, giant, and obstacle that I'm faced with. You wouldn't give me a mission I couldn't conquer, so I will courageously go forth and possess the land.

In Jesus' name, Amen.

Be Yourself

Am I now trying to win the approval of human beings, or of God?
Or am I trying to please people? If I were still trying to please people,
I would not be a servant of Christ.

Galatians 1:10, NIV

God made you the way you are for a reason: you have something that the world needs to see, hear, and feel. God doesn't want you to try to be someone else or attempt to obtain what He has for you by doing things the way you see others doing them. God wants you to act, speak, sing, write, play, preach, teach, parent, and do more, the way that *you* do it. He doesn't want you to mimic someone else's success.

There will be people you look up to and admire, but you must still realize that your path is different from theirs. God didn't make you different in order for you to become a replica of someone else. He wants you to pave your own way, make your own lane, and stay in it with Him. Everyone won't understand or support you, but as long as you have God's approval, you have all you need, so just be yourself.

You will be surprised who's watching and gravitating towards your light. God blesses you for being who He called you to be and remaining true to your character. Doing this in a world that beckons for you to be just like everyone else requires boldness and tenacity that comes from being firmly rooted in your relationship with God. He can't bless an imposter—who you pretend or try to be—because that isn't the real you. When you are yourself, God will open doors for you that no one can shut. He will make it possible for you to obtain what He said is yours, even if He has to make a way in the wilderness or a river in the desert. He just needs for you to be you.

Remember that you are enough, and you don't have to figure out how God's plan will unfold in your life. Don't worry about the next person or how it happened for them. God is writing your story, too, and it will be unlike anything you've heard or seen happen for anyone else because God loves to surprise us.

Remember, God can't bless who you pretend to be. Since God already loves and accepts you for who you are, why try to be anyone else? God created you in His image and He is so proud of you. He longs to use you to show off His power but it requires you to embrace the beautiful, brave, special, and remarkable human being He made when He formed you.

Being yourself does not mean that you shouldn't change, it simply means that even in the process of growing, changing, and evolving, you're just becoming an even better version of who God already made you to be. As He fine tunes you to perfection, don't try to fit inside someone else's definition of who you should be. Refuse to take on roles, characteristics, or habits that persuade you to compromise your character. You're better than that. You are called to be different and set apart for God's purpose. Will you let Him use you—the real you—to draw others to Him?

Reflect and Pray

No longer will I shrink myself to fit where I simply do not belong. I will be myself because that's who God wants to use.

Lord, thank You for making me who I am. Thank you for loving the things that other people may dislike or frown upon. Please help me to embrace myself entirely and mold me further into who You have called me to be so that I can fulfill my purpose in Your Kingdom.

In Jesus' name, Amen.

Be Giving

For if the intention and desire are there, the size of the gift doesn't matter.
Your gift is fully acceptable to God according to what you have,
not what you don't have.

2 Corinthians 8:12, TPT

When you give, it should be with joyous expectation. Luke 6:38 says "give, and it will be given to you" (ESV), so we should be looking for God to bless us in some way for our obedience. We give to please God and bring glory to His name, but we cannot please Him if we give begrudgingly. Second Corinthians 9:7 says, "God loves a cheerful giver" (ESV). So the act of giving itself, or the amount of what you give, is not nearly as important as the *attitude* of your heart when you give.

When we think of the word, "give," we typically think of money, but we give in other ways, too. We give of our time, effort, and energy, such as love, attention, and affection. For example, when you volunteer, you are giving your time, effort, and energy to a cause that is bigger than yourself, but sometimes in the midst of giving ourselves to our jobs, relationships, hobbies, responsibilities, and everything else, we forget the most important thing: *giving should begin with God.* And God doesn't want the *most*, He wants the *best*. You give God your best by giving Him first place in every area of your life. God wants first dibs, not what's left over after everyone else has had their fill. He knows when your efforts are half-hearted, lackluster, or misguided.

The same rules apply when it comes to giving to God by blessing the church. Don't give just because it's in the Word or because you want God to do something for you in exchange. Give your best. Give because you love God. Give because He's already done so much for you. Give because you want to be a blessing to God's house. Give because you want to be a part of what God is doing in your church's outreach ministries throughout the community.

To be giving, you have to learn to think of others more than you think of yourself. It's easy to do things for yourself, but when was the last time you did something for someone else—not on a birthday, holiday, or anniversary, but *just because?* A good giver is loving, humble, people-oriented, and sincere. She is not motivated by selfish gain, but she is after the heart of God—who *so loved* the world that He *gave* His only Son (John 3:16, ESV).

God gave us His best in order to set the example that every time we give, we should do the same. God is not concerned about what you don't have, but how you give what you do have. The next time you give, give your best. Give happily, humbly, and eagerly. Your best worship. Your best praise. Your best offering. Your best gift. Your best hug. Your best smile. Your best effort.

Examine your intentions when it comes to giving and remember that everything you do is really for God. Are you only giving to receive, or because you feel obligated? Or are you giving your *best?*

Reflect and Pray

No longer will I give begrudgingly or out of obligation or selfishness. I will be a cheerful giver who gives her best.

Lord, thank You for blessing me to be a giver. Please help me to give my best in everything I do, knowing that it is really You I am doing it for.

In Jesus' name, Amen.

Be Still

"Be still, and know that I am God. I will be exalted among the nations,
I will be exalted in the earth!"

Psalm 46:10, ESV

Imagine being in a season of your life when you were waiting on a response from or an act of God. Whether you're looking for God to give you direction on your next steps, to supply a financial need, or to perform a miracle in your family, you cast your cares upon the Lord and wait patiently for Him to move.

Days or weeks later, you're still waiting for that answer from God. Worry drops by your door, discouragement starts to creep in, and you begin to fight to hold on to the hope that filled your heart when you first believed. You're doing everything you can to hold on, but if you're honest, your faith is steadily dwindling away.

Maybe you don't have to imagine. Maybe like the disciples in Mark 4, you're in the boat right now, wondering when God will calm the wind, when He will tame the storm, or if He even cares that you're drowning at all. It's hard to trust a God who says He is with you but feels absent when you need Him the most. It's hard to be still when the world around you is not.

Yet, that's exactly what God tells us to do: *"be still and know that I am God"* (Psalm 46:10 NIV). This stillness that God is calling us to is not inaction, but surrender—yielding our concerns to God and allowing Him to be who He promised us He is, even when it means fighting the urge to take matters into our own hands and do something because we think God is taking too long.

There are times when you need an answer by a certain date, and as the deadline approaches your mind begins to entertain the idea of another option, crafting a way to secure your future because you think God is somewhere twiddling His thumbs, unconcerned with whatever's concerning you.

Instead, what if we challenge ourselves to believe that God is who He says He is, and will do what He says He will do? What if instead of plotting a way out, a plan B, or an escape route, we take our fleeting faith to God and like the ruler who asked Jesus to heal his daughter say, "I believe; help my unbelief!" (Mark 9:24, ESV).

You don't have to rely on your own strength to believe. Lean on God and allow Him to not only be the miracle-working God, but also the faith-preserving One. Hope in the Lord and wait for Him to act. Hold your peace because God gave it to you. Be still and know that He is God. While you are still, He's on the move.

Reflect and Pray

No longer will I be quick to move when I'm waiting for God to act. I will be still and wait for God to move, trusting that He will come through in time.

Lord, thank You for being the God who hears and sees me. Thank you that You have never forsaken me and are with me, even when I can't see or understand what You're doing. Help me to be still and trust that You are in control and that my future is secure in You.

In Jesus' name, Amen.

Be Thankful

Let everything that has breath praise the LORD! Praise the LORD!

Psalm 150:6, ESV

Have you ever complained so much that you got tired of hearing your own voice? The more you dwelled on your issues, the more frustrated you became. When you complain, you not only remain in your situation, but you sink into a weak and unproductive state mentally and emotionally because you're only thinking about yourself and the negative.

Being thankful is an attitude and a choice. It doesn't mean you aren't expecting God to do bigger and greater things, as you should. It simply means that no matter what state you find yourself in, your mindset is focused on God and giving Him praise, knowing the best is yet to come. A person who is thankful is happy, joyful, and at peace—even in the midst of chaos or turmoil.

When you feel the urge to complain, speak gratitude instead. Begin to thank God for everything He has done, is doing, and is going to do in your life. Think back to when you prayed for what you have now and give God thanks that He manifested those things. It's going to get better, but here, in this in-between phase, in this imperfect place, in this seemingly dry and weary desert, the gratitude that you give God now shows Him that *your season does not determine your praise.* Your humble heart of thankfulness will only cause God to bless you even more because He knows you love and appreciate Him for *who He is.*

When unfortunate life-altering events occur, such as suffering from a chronic disease or losing someone close to you, it can be incredibly difficult to still give God praise. That is why Paul tells us: "No matter what happens, *always* be thankful, for this is God's will for you who belong to Christ Jesus" (1 Thessalonians 5:18, TLB). When you are *always* thankful, you build up a resolve deep within your soul that is determined to glorify God regardless of how you feel. So when those painful, frightening situations arise and shift your world completely, they will not cause you to lose faith in God. Even if your hope is hanging on by a thread, you will still be able to give God glory because you know that He is strengthening and sustaining you, bearing the magnitude of what is hurting you.

Sometimes things just don't happen how or when we want them to, but our unmet expectations or desires are not reasons to deny God His praise. As the popular saying goes, "He's still God, and He's still good©" (lyrics by Lake, Quilala, & Smith, 1971).

True thankfulness is independent of circumstance. It doesn't matter what you're going through right now, your well of gratitude should always be overflowing with surrender to an everlasting God who holds your heart in His hands. He has not forgotten or forsaken you; He is with you. God is near to the brokenhearted and saves the crushed in spirit (Psalm 34:18, ESV). And no matter what it looks like right now, it could always be worse, so just be thankful.

Reflect and Pray

No longer will I focus on my problems and forsake giving my Creator the praise He deserves. In every circumstance, I will be thankful.

Lord, I just want to say thank You. Thank You for who You are. Thank You for everything You have done for me. Thank You for loving, forgiving, covering, and choosing me. Thank You for what You're doing in my life.

In Jesus' name, Amen.

WHATEVER IS RIGHT

Choose God's will. Surrender everything else.

Living a just—righteous, upstanding—life requires radical intentionality. There will always be a choice between right and wrong, what *feels* right and what *is* right, what seems good to us and what is God's will for us. In each scenario we must purpose in our minds to choose the right thing—the thing that is pleasing in God's sight—instead of the thing that satisfies our flesh in the moment. As daughters of God, it should be our goal to get closer to Him daily so that when we meet a fork in the road, we'll choose to make the right decision, even if the consequences are difficult to deal with.

Everyone won't support or understand the decisions you make as a daughter of God. Standing on God's Word and choosing His will for your life certainly comes with a price. It may cost you friends, opportunities, and money. But the Word says, "And everyone who has given up houses or brothers or sisters or father or mother or children or property, for my sake, will receive a hundred times as much in return and will inherit eternal life" (Matthew 19:29, NLT). In other words, there's nothing you give up for God that He won't return to you, and in excess. Still, it can be a difficult path to walk.

Choosing right (God's will) from wrong (everything else) is hard because so many factors weigh into our decisions—how we feel, how it affects us and those around us, and what life will look like as a result of that decision. It can also be tough to choose right in the heat of the moment when we have to make a quick decision. The battle between pleasing God or keeping the peace isn't always easily won, but we can be comforted by the fact that God is "working in you, giving you the desire and the power to do what pleases him" (Philippians 2:13, NLT).

Jesus is our example of what it means to choose whatever is right. Despite temptation, He always chose the righteous path, even though He knew He would be judged, rejected, and persecuted for His decisions. He showed us how to make decisions that were pleasing in God's sight, despite how others responded to His decisions. He knew ultimately that what mattered most was accomplishing the purpose God sent Him to Earth to fulfill.

You won't always get it right, and that's ok. What matters is that you strive to draw closer to God each day so that your desires will line up with His perfect will for your life, making it easier both to serve Him and to say no to anything that conflicts with His predestined purpose for you.

It won't always be easy. It won't always feel good. But I'm determined to make the right decisions, even if it means surrendering what's more convenient for me at the time. I'm not here for my own pleasure or satisfaction. I was created to please the Lord.

Choose Obedience

As obedient children, do not be conformed to the passions of your former ignorance, but as he who called you is holy, you also be holy in all your conduct, since it is written, 'You shall be holy, for I am holy.'

1 Peter 1: 14-16, ESV

Obedience is a huge theme throughout the Bible. As a daughter of God who's getting to know Him better, you may wonder why that is.

When we obey God, we show Him that fulfilling His will is more important to us than our own desires, and that we are willing to forsake what we want in order to live out His good and perfect purpose for our lives.

Obedience matters because God's will for your life fits into a much bigger scheme and plan, and that is God's desire for "all people to be saved and to come to the knowledge of the truth" (1 Timothy 2:4, ESV). You have a major role to play in this! By sharing your testimony, witnessing to others, and giving your life as a living sacrifice for God to use, you make it possible for others to see and know Him.

Obedience requires an immense amount of self-sacrifice—denying yourself what you really want. There will be places you want to go and God will say no; opportunities you want to pursue and God will lead you in a different direction; people you want to be close to that God will discourage you from befriending, etc. It can be tough to walk in obedience, especially if others around you are not called to the same level of responsibility and accountability that God is now requiring of you. God will *always* reward your obedience with His goodness, for "blessed rather are those who hear the word of God and keep it!" (Luke 11:28, ESV).

It is the Holy Spirit—God's Spirit that dwells inside us—that informs us when we are headed in the wrong direction. It's so tempting to do what feels good at the moment. The Good News is that God doesn't just expect us to make the right decision when we are faced with the temptation to please our flesh. The Word says that "...God is faithful, and he will not let you be tempted beyond your ability, but with the temptation he will also provide the way of escape, that you may be able to endure it" (1 Corinthians 10:13, ESV).

God knows what's best for you, and His plans for you are for good, not disaster, to give you a future and a hope (Jeremiah 29:11). Trust Him to help you walk out His good and perfect will for your life.

Reflect and Pray

I surrender the urge to only do what seems and feels right to me in the moment. I choose to obey God, even when it means denying myself, because He knows what's best for me and His plans for me are good.

Lord, thank You for creating me for a purpose and a time such as this. Please order my steps and help me to lead a life of obedience that is pleasing to You and in accordance with Your plans for my life.

In Jesus' name, Amen.

Choose Trust

But blessed are those who trust in the Lord and have made the Lord their hope and confidence. They are like trees planted along a riverbank, with roots that reach deep into the water. Such trees are not bothered by the heat or worried by long months of drought. Their leaves stay green, and they never stop producing fruit.

Jeremiah 17:7-8, NLT

Trusting in God is something we're often encouraged to do, but trusting God is a process—and learning how to trust Him isn't easy at first.

When you trust God it means you fully rely on Him, which means you depend on His power, strength, knowledge, ability, etc. over of your own. It's hard to do that—especially if you're used to depending on yourself. Trusting God is all-consuming and requires that we completely allow Him to be Lord over our lives and our decisions. It's a total freefall. And that is *scary*.

It's scary because our natural human inclination is to *doubt*. We doubt not because God's track record isn't proven, but because either we don't have a history of trusting God to fall back on, or because we've reached new, uncharted territory with God that's made trusting hard. No matter what season you're in with God, it not only requires the faith to believe that He can, but also the assurance to know that no matter the outcome, it will be for your good.

Your reality today is that you're afraid to trust God. Know that it's okay. Your unbelief is not foreign to God, nor is it a problem for Him. Rather, it's an opportunity for you to lean into the discomfort of the unknown and allow God to prove to you, once again, that He cannot and will not fail you.

There's a story in Mark 9:14-29 about a man whose son had a spirit that made him unable to speak. After Jesus told the man to bring the boy to him, the father said, "If you can do anything, have compassion on us and help us," to which Jesus replied, "'If you can'! All things are possible for one who believes.'" After hearing this, the father cries out to Jesus, "I believe; help my unbelief!" and Jesus cast the spirit out of the boy.

This story is a reminder that even when you desperately want to believe and trust God but just can't fully relinquish your doubt, He will still come through for you. Don't let the point of your unbelief push you away from God. Give it to Him and He will help you trust Him.

Trust doesn't come naturally at first, but the more you let go of your need to be in control of the outcome and give God a chance to show you He's worthy of your trust, the more He will show up in your life in ways you could never have imagined He would.

Reflect and Pray

I surrender my need to know, understand, plan, or control everything. I choose to trust God with my life because He is capable and faithful to perform.

Lord, teach me how to trust You even when I don't know or understand what You are doing. Help me to rest in Your promises, knowing You care for me and everything that concerns me. Thank You for allowing me the space to grow in my faith as I get closer to You each day.

In Jesus' name, Amen.

Choose Integrity

People with integrity walk safely, but those who follow crooked paths will be exposed.

Proverbs 10:9, NLT

Who are you in the absence of accountability? Do you still represent God the same way you would in the presence of your godly friends, family members, or fellow churchgoers? Or does your presentation change?

Don't get me wrong—accountability matters. It is essential to our walk with God to have parents, friends, spouses, pastors, and others who help us "stay on the straight and narrow," open our eyes to our shortcomings, and point us back to Jesus. What happens when it's just you? Are you still able to uphold godly morals and values, or do you compromise because there's no one there to keep the score? That's where integrity comes in.

Integrity is being honest, truthful, and loyal to your moral principles, and being upright in character and actions. So walking in integrity means living out what it is you say you believe—honoring God in both your words and your deeds. As a daughter of God looking to be a light in a world full of darkness, integrity *matters.*

In this technologically advanced society we live in, it seems as if anything you do and say is recorded, screenshotted, shared, and reshared. Even if it's not, it's important to remember that someone is always watching—and that someone is God. How we live out our life before Him and others counts for something, both in this life and the next. When you lack integrity, it's easy to fall prey to the cycle of living for the moment rather than for eternity, making excuses for your behavior rather than homing in on your weaknesses and actively working to change those behaviors that push you further from God.

You may be in an environment at school or in the workplace where the people around you don't live by the same standards as you, and therefore would give you a pass if you exemplified qualities that aren't Christlike. As a daughter of God, you are a light bearer, and you may be the only glimmer of God that they see. Instead of blending in just because no one's calling you out on your actions, aim to please the Father in everything you do. As Paul advises us in Romans 12:2, "Do not be shaped by this world; instead, be changed within by a new way of thinking. Then you will be able to decide what God wants for you; you will know what is good and pleasing to him and what is perfect" (NCV). Don't lose your stand. Since it is against God that we sin—work to change those habits and behaviors that don't honor Him so you can best represent Him.

Some people think that because they haven't committed certain sins or don't have a sinful past that they have integrity, but that isn't necessarily the case. Integrity isn't about perfection or even "doing right." Integrity is about *being holy*. For the Word says, "Be ye holy; for I am holy" (1 Peter 1:16, KJV). So keep in mind that upholding a standard out of obligation or a need to prove your character to someone (even if that someone is yourself) is not integrity but a form of pride. Integrity is rooted in a genuine desire to be righteous and more like Christ every day because you love God and want to please Him, not because you want to show others how good and holy you are.

In the same way that David prayed, "Search me, O God, and know my heart: try me, and know my thoughts: And see if there be any wicked way in me, and lead me in the way everlasting," (Psalm 139:23-24, KJV), we should humble ourselves and allow God to point our attention towards those places in our lives where we need to be more like Him. No matter where this devotional found you, you can recommit yourself today to leading a life that is honorable before Him.

Reflect and Pray

I surrender the urge to only "do right" when someone's watching or holding me accountable. I choose to live holy because I want to please the Father, not man.

Lord, thank You for revealing to me areas where I am lacking in integrity. Help me to lay aside everything that hinders my walk with You so that I can be more like You and a better example to those I am called to.

In Jesus' name, Amen.

Choose Forgiveness

Then Peter came up and said to him, "Lord, how often will my brother sin against me, and I forgive him? As many as seven times?" Jesus said to him, "I do not say to you seven times, but seventy-seven times.

Matthew 18:21-22, ESV

Have you ever been wronged so badly by someone that you didn't know how, when, or even if you could forgive them? Forgiveness is one of the fundamental principles of our faith, but it's also one of the toughest things to do when we've been hurt or betrayed, especially by someone we dearly loved.

It's crucial to forgive because the Bible says, "For if you forgive others their trespasses, your heavenly Father will also forgive you, but if you do not forgive others their trespasses, neither will your Father forgive your trespasses" (Matthew 6:14-15, ESV). Forgiveness is understandably not the first thing on our minds when a person deeply wounds us. Sometimes you aren't ready to get over it, and because you know that God desires you to forgive, you might be inclined to back off from spending time with Him. When you are hurt or offended, the best thing you can do is turn toward the Father, not away from Him. You don't have to hide your hurt from God. Let Him meet you in your time of need and minister to the parts of your heart that need healing.

Sometimes forgiveness is even harder because of our triggers or past traumas. There will even be times in your life where forgiving yourself is harder than forgiving someone else. In these situations, it's good to talk to a therapist—particularly a Christian one—they will help you work through the situation and give you tools and exercises to grapple with your emotions rather than tuck them away.

On that note, be sure to seek out a therapist who is trained in your area of need, who you connect with, and is a good fit for you. Trust God to direct you to the right therapist and use the first session or two to determine if your therapist makes you feel seen, heard, and challenged before you continue working with them.

Ultimately, unforgiveness is a thief that robs you of peace, joy, and the ability and freedom to fully execute your God-given purpose. It usually starts with allowing anger to fester, to *linger.* That's why the Word says, "If you are angry, don't sin by nursing your grudge. Don't let the sun go down with you still angry—get over it quickly" (Ephesians 4:26, TLB). What you don't confront cannot be resolved. So when a friend hurts or offends you, it's important to talk it over with them, but first, pray that God will not only guide you in what to say, but also in how to say it, *when* to say it, and that the conflict will get resolved.

Forgiving doesn't mean you have to allow someone back into close relationship with you. It means that what happened no longer angers you, nor do you hold it against the person. For the Word says, "Be kind to one another, tenderhearted, forgiving one another, as God in Christ forgave you" (Ephesians 4:32, ESV).

Forgiveness is one of the fruits of the Spirit (Galatians 5:22-23), which means that the closer we get to God, the easier it becomes to forgive. Apart from God, our hearts can become so hard that forgiveness isn't even an option. When we spend time with Him, casting our cares upon Him and allowing Him to move in our hearts, we become more ready and able to forgive.

Last, remember that forgiveness is often a decision before it is a feeling. It's a choice to let a person off the hook, even when we know just how wrong what they did was. We can take comfort in the fact that "while we were still sinners, Christ died for us" (Romans 5:8, NIV). Jesus is the ultimate example of forgiveness. Not only did He forgive us, but He laid down His life for us, bearing the burden and shame of our sin that we could live freely in Him.

Remember there will be times when you, too, will need forgiveness. So don't live offended. Allow forgiveness into your heart and move forward in love.

Reflect and Pray

I surrender the tendency to nurse grudges and allow hurt, anger, and unforgiveness to go unresolved. I choose to follow the example of Christ and take the necessary steps to forgive those who have hurt and offended me.

Lord, thank You for pointing my attention to individuals I have yet to forgive, and those areas in my heart where I still need to be healed. Please heal me from the hurt that person caused and help me to walk in forgiveness so that I can love them completely.

In Jesus' name, Amen.

Choose Grace

Let us then with confidence draw near to the throne of grace,
that we may receive mercy and find grace to help in time of need.

Hebrews 4:16, ESV

Forgiveness and grace go hand in hand, as forgiving requires us to extend grace—understanding that people fall short, and allowing them room to be human, and to grow.

Grace is the unmerited favor of God. We don't deserve it, we didn't earn it, but He still shines His face upon us. Grace is a courtesy, a kindness that you extend to others out of the overflow of love God has given you. Extending grace means looking beyond their actions or attitude and loving them enough to give them the opportunity to grow past this moment. Just as God gives us grace, we honor Him by doing the same for others.

In doing so, you can't hold everyone in your life to the same standard because everyone isn't in the same place mentally, spiritually, physically, or emotionally. You also cannot assume someone "knows better" if you haven't had that conversation with them. Give people the opportunity to love you well and to do right by you. If and when they repeatedly don't, adjust accordingly, but don't make it a habit of cutting people off for minor offenses when God placed that person in your life for a purpose, or perhaps placed you in their life for a purpose.

Some relationships won't always be mutually beneficial. Be willing to be a friend if God is asking that of you, even when that person doesn't have the capacity to be a friend back to you. Open your eyes and see the opportunity God has created for you to grow in love and grace. There may be a season when they can reciprocate what you've poured into them, but even if there isn't, know that God is pleased because you did it unto Him. By extending grace you're allowing God's light to shine through you; this is yet another way to witness to someone.

Now, offering grace does not mean allowing someone to mistreat or disrespect you, which you should never tolerate. There's also grace in walking away and allowing that person the space they need to grow and heal. In situations when you've been wronged and are justifiably offended, grace will help keep you from dragging that person's name through the mud. Hold your head up high and know that vengeance belongs to God.

Grace is hard to give when you attempt to pour out of your own ability. The closer you get to the Father the easier it will become to pardon others, to offer understanding for their situation, and to love them beyond their shortcomings. That's grace.

Reflect and Pray

I surrender the idea of "matching energy." I choose to extend grace and allow others the room they need to grow and heal.

Lord, thank You for revealing to me the areas where I need to extend others more grace. Forgive me for my lack of understanding and help me to offer them the same grace You have kindly extended towards me.

In Jesus' name, Amen.

Choose Silence

"Be silent before the Lord and wait expectantly for him . . ."

Psalm 37:7, CSB

Our world is loud. At work, at school, at home, on television or on social media—wherever you go—there's always something or someone vying for your attention. With everything you're pursuing and responsible for, it can be hard to turn it all off so you can spend time with God.

It's hard to hear from God when we won't silence the noise around us or in our minds. God always wants to speak to us—to give us direction on our next steps, to reveal a heart change we need to make, or just to tell us how much He loves us. We can't hear from Him if we don't make room for Him.

Whether we're willing to admit it or not, I believe that sometimes we don't pray and spend time with God because we think it's a waste of time. You know that if you pour into your business, it will flourish. If you pour into your family, love will flow. If you pour into your career, you'll (eventually) get the job, promotion, or opportunity you're hoping for. If you pour into the gym, your dream body will slowly reveal itself. Why is it that we don't see being alone with our Father as the most productive way we can invest our time?

I believe it's because we don't believe the result will be tangible or immediate, and when we want something from God, when we're believing Him for a miracle, or when we've hit rock bottom, we make sure He hears us. God craves a relationship with us that isn't based on our needs and that requires us to quiet the noise.

Jesus knew this. And it's why He went away to pray—not just when He was hurting, like after John the Baptist was beheaded (Matthew 14:1-13), or when He was in anguish, like when He prayed in the garden of Gethsemane shortly before enduring the Cross (Matthew 26:36-56), but Jesus made a lifestyle habit of getting alone to be with God without distractions. He set this example for His disciples to follow.

Likewise, we should choose silence. Choose to escape the noise. Choose to wait patiently before the Lord. Sit in the silence. Sit with expectation. Share what's on your heart. There, in the stillness, allow God to meet you where you are. He will not disappoint.

Reflect and Pray

I surrender the tendency to neglect spending time alone with God because it is uncomfortable or inconvenient. I choose to silence the noise and make time for my Father.

Lord, thank You for desiring to spend quality time with me, away from the cares of this world and the demands of this life. Please forgive me for not honoring my sacred time with You. From this day forward I commit to prioritizing time with You over tackling my to-do list.

In Jesus' name, Amen.

Choose Joy

A joyful heart is good medicine, but a crushed spirit dries up the bones.

Proverbs 17:22, ESV

When we look at the current state of our world, it seems the fight for joy has never been so strong. From the constant negative reports we see on the news to what we're presented on social media, to the difficulties we face in our daily lives, holding onto our joy presents a significant challenge for us as believers. There will be moments when you feel like the weight of the world is pressing in on you; it feels as if the air has been seized from your lungs because things are just that hopeless. When it feels like despair, misfortune, and negativity surround us, we need a place of refuge from the calamity that drains us of our joy and therefore, our strength.

The presence of the Lord is that refuge. Psalm 16:11 says, "You make known to me the path of life; in your presence there is fullness of joy; at your right hand are pleasures forevermore" (ESV). Joy is a feeling of pleasure and contentment that isn't rooted in what you have but rather in the confidence that all is well, no matter what you do or don't have. That confidence can only come from knowing and trusting in God. True, endless, and abounding joy is a natural byproduct of a relationship with God. His joy is everlasting. His joy is full, boundless, and eternal. When we live in His presence and allow His Spirit to dwell within us, we always have access to this priceless joy.

Having the joy of the Lord doesn't mean that everything is going the way you want it to, but that in spite of what's happening you can still be content, at peace, happy, and hopeful because you know God is your source and strength.

Having joy does not mean denying or ignoring your pain. It's important to recognize, identify and hold space for every emotion we feel—sadness, grief, anger, disappointment—but we don't have to remain in a state of despair. We can choose to give God our burdens in exchange for His joy. Joy is not a band-aid, it's a remedy—one that we can only find in the arms and presence of our Father.

You deserve to experience a joy that fills your soul and flows into everything you do. Know that the devil, your adversary, hates it when you experience such joy. He comes to "kill, steal, and destroy" and that includes your joy and every other fruit of the Spirit that is your portion—love, peace, patience, kindness, goodness, faithfulness, gentleness, and self-control (Galatians 5:22-23). But Jesus came for us to have life, and to have it more abundantly (John 10:10). And that abundant life includes joy.

Don't let the enemy take a gift from you that came directly from God, your Creator. God created you with joy for you to experience a joyful life in Him. He wants to satisfy you with the fullness of joy that awaits you in His presence. He, too, is grieved by your despair, trials, and trauma. He is moved by what moves you. He is near to you in your broken-heartedness and longs to trade your sorrow for His gift of joy and contentment. When you find yourself in the middle of a storm, remember that choosing joy doesn't mean avoiding the weight of your emotions. What you feel is valid and God is with you, even in your sadness and discouragement.

So acknowledge it. Feel it. Then, cast your cares upon the Lord. He cares for you, and He will make your heart light once again.

Reflect and Pray

I surrender the habit of denying my feelings in an effort to have joy. I choose to acknowledge my emotions and allow God to bear the burden of my pain so that I can live in His joy.

Lord, thank You for allowing me access to joy—a God-given gift of contentment that remains with me in spite of what's happening in my life. Thank You that I can choose to have joy no matter what's going on around me. Help me to remain in this state of confident pleasure and delight in You.

In Jesus' name, Amen.

Choose Faith

And without faith it is impossible to please him, for whoever would draw near to God must believe that he exists and that he rewards those who seek him.

Hebrews 11:6, ESV

Choosing faith is often a fight, especially if you're used to depending on yourself or others' ability to make things happen instead of God's. If you've ever believed God for something big and scary, you know that it takes determination to believe because your faith will be threatened. Questioned. Stirred. Tested. Shaken.

Sometimes having faith will feel like walking on water. Sometimes having faith will feel like drowning in that same water, but in either situation, God is present and He is your help. He'll help you trust Him when it's the hardest thing you've ever done. He'll help your unbelief.

Choosing to have faith stretches you to forsake your inclination to figure it out yourself, "make a way," or even give up and instead, wait patiently for God to act with the confidence that He will. We have to trust that even if God doesn't move the way we hoped or believed He would, He's still able, He's still God, He's still worthy of our worship. Romans 8:28 assures us that whatever outcome He brings us to, He is a good God who works all things together for our good. Through maturing in our relationship with God, we can grow to always seek God and have faith for Him to act, not just when we don't have it within our power to change the situation.

Having faith does not mean waiting idly by for God to act. It means moving with intention and trusting that He will guide your steps. For example, if you're believing God for a new job, you don't just wait around hoping you'll randomly get a call when you haven't even put yourself out there. You perfect your resume, apply for positions, network, and continue developing your skills. You don't know how God will do it but faith is active, not dormant. Make preparations for what you're believing for God to do.

All throughout Scripture you will encounter testimonies of the faithfulness of God. In your own life; if you look back, you can see what the Lord has done. You can see how He has kept you. He made a way when there didn't seem a way could be made. He brought you through the toughest seasons of your life.

Your faith isn't built on mere hope, but it's built on a God who has proven Himself worthy of our complete trust and obedience. Not once has He failed you. Not once has He fallen short of His word. Not once has He stopped being God, the Sufficient One, the One who makes all things new and who is not only capable, but faithful to perform. He's done enough. He *is* enough.

Having faith in God is a lifelong journey but your faith will never fail you when it's in a God who doesn't fail. Put Him to the test and watch Him work. Over and over again, He always comes through.

Reflect and Pray

I surrender my need to be in control of every outcome. I choose to have faith in God's ability to perform because He knows what's best for me.

Lord, thank You that You want to order my steps, and that Your plans for me are good. Help me to have faith in Your ability to act. Help me to follow You without fear that You will let me down. I know that You won't fail.

In Jesus' name, Amen.

Choose Honesty

Do not lie to one another, seeing that you have put off the old self with its practices and have put on the new self, which is being renewed in knowledge after the image of its creator.

Colossians 3:9-10, ESV

If you ever learned the phrase, "honesty is the best policy," as a child, you likely encountered a situation later in life that put this assertion to the test.

Not to say that it isn't true, because it is. Honesty is good, right, appropriate, and pleasing to God, but what this phrase lacks is *parameters*. There's a place, a time, and a way to be honest. It begins with being honest with yourself.

We seem to be more eager to highlight or discuss others' shortcomings than we are to turn the mirror on ourselves and examine our own flaws and areas in need of improvement. Jesus talks about this in Matthew 7:3-5: "Why do you see the speck that is in your brother's eye, but do not notice the log that is in your own eye? Or how can you say to your brother, 'Let me take the speck out of your eye,' when there is the log in your own eye? You hypocrite, first take the log out of your own eye, and then you will see clearly to take the speck out of your brother's eye" (ESV).

Before taking the opportunity to tell others about their issues, we need to make sure we've taken time for self-reflection, as David does in Psalm 139:23-24 when he prays, "Search me, O God, and know my heart! Try me and know my thoughts! And see if there be any grievous way in me, and lead me in the way everlasting!" (ESV). When we have done that, our truth will likely be better received.

In being honest, it's important to first seek the Lord. There will be times when you're the one God is trusting to reveal something to another person but how and when to be honest is determined by both the leading of the Holy

Spirit and your relationship with that person. Proximity to a person will not only help guide your words, but also your tone. You probably wouldn't speak to your parents or pastor the same way you would to your spouse or best friend. Know your audience and aim to be like Christ in how you handle conversations.

In relationships, conflict arises. Sometimes it's good to talk things over with a close friend who will give you godly wisdom or even your therapist before you attempt to resolve the situation. Honesty does not have to be harsh. So in being honest, also be respectful. Be kind. Be mindful that the person you're talking to is a daughter or child of God as well. She or he is also an image bearer of God who also deserves kindness, mercy, and grace. It's important to come from a place of love, respect, and honor when you're telling a person the truth—especially about themselves—because while the truth sets us free, it isn't always easy to receive.

As a daughter and disciple of God, know that your approach matters. Your delivery alone can make or break whether or not a person receives from you. Don't miss your opportunity to minister or get through to someone because you aren't willing to be wise about how you package the truth.

So choose honesty but lead with love.

Reflect and Pray

I surrender the haste to tell others about themselves before examining myself. I choose to be honest in a way that is loving, kind, and considerate of the other person.

Lord, thank You for showing me areas I need to address before I attempt to correct others. Help me to be honest with myself and others without judgment but in love.

In Jesus' name, Amen.

Choose Discipline

I discipline my body like an athlete, training it to do what it should. Otherwise,
I fear that after preaching to others I myself might be disqualified.

1 Corinthians 9:27, NLT

"I don't feel like it."

How many times have you uttered this statement and not done the thing you committed to do or know you need to? Whether it's spiritual: getting up early to pray; reading your Bible; staying dedicated to your fast; or physical: exercising; drinking more water; or relational: showing up for a friend; or personal: executing a task related to your calling, etc. We all have a number of responsibilities and goals we're working towards that require a level of discipline for us to follow through. Discipline is uncomfortable, inconvenient, and even frustrating at times because it forces you to reject what your body naturally *wants* to do and instead, command yourself to do what you've set your mind to do.

Nothing you desire or that God has commissioned you to do will get accomplished without discipline. While it isn't the easy choice, it's the best one for us because it will ultimately put us in a better position, which is always God's will for us, if we stick with it. As Hebrews 12:11 says, "For the moment all discipline seems painful rather than pleasant, but later it yields the peaceful fruit of righteousness to those who have been trained by it" (ESV).

Another challenging aspect of discipline is not only having to say no to yourself, but also saying it to others. There will be times when what your friend or even your spouse wants to do will be in direct conflict with what you've committed to do. For example, if you're disciplining yourself to go to the gym every day at 5 am, it takes discipline to get out of the bed and go when you look over and see your husband is still peacefully sleeping. If you're working towards a financial goal, it takes discipline not to swipe your card and get those new shoes when you're out with friends.

Learning to tell our flesh, "No" rather than doing what we feel like doing in the moment is godly and necessary. Not only does discipline allow us the opportunity to accomplish our goals, but also it brings us closer to God as we deny what our flesh naturally wants in exchange for feeding our spirit, the part of us that yearns to commune with and be more like Christ.

When you choose discipline, you won't get it right every day, but each month you can choose 2-3 habits or goals you want to focus on and develop discipline in those areas over time. It's also good to fast periodically as the Lord leads you to (such as at the beginning of the month or once every quarter) to keep your flesh under control. Over time, it will become easier to choose the things of God and complete the tasks that will create a better life and future for you rather than what will satisfy you in the moment.

Reflect and Pray

I surrender the natural, fleshly inclination to only do what I feel like doing. I choose to discipline myself so that I can accomplish my spiritual, personal, relational and financial goals.

Lord, thank You for revealing to me the areas where I need to become more disciplined in order to obtain what I truly desire. Help me to discipline my flesh and lean into my spirit in order to become more committed in achieving what I set out to do.

In Jesus' name, Amen.

Choose Rest

And he said to them, "Come away by yourselves to a desolate place and rest a while." For many were coming and going, and they had no leisure even to eat.

Mark 6:3, ESV

Grind. Hustle. Go harder. Do more.

These days it seems countless podcasters, coaches, and gurus push this mentality of working nonstop until you get to where you want to be. Hustle culture will tell you that being successful requires doing whatever it takes to get there—getting up early, staying up late, and putting all your efforts into your career or business-related pursuits. Throughout social media you'll encounter influencers, business owners and entrepreneurs who push the narrative that you have to show up every day, outwork your competitors, and only rest on holidays (if then) in order to win. You don't stop until you've reached your goals. Then, you set another goal. It's an endless work cycle that leaves no room for gratitude or contentment.

Let me be clear: I am not implying that we should abandon working hard in pursuit of the extreme opposite—laziness—for the Bible says, "Lazy people want much but get little, but those who work hard will prosper" (Proverbs 13:4, NLT). Indeed, having a focused, committed work ethic that allows you to enjoy financial security and freedom is *good*.

No work ethic is *godly* if it lacks the essential component of rest and sometimes we prioritize productivity over rest when we don't fully trust that God will take care of us. We push ourselves to the brink of burnout because we think that if we don't, we'll never reach our financial goals or create the lives we want for ourselves.

Without rest, our pursuits are misguided and fruitless because we will lack the mental and physical endurance we need for the journey. Oftentimes we put off rest because we see it as an unnecessary use of our time when it really is what enables us to make the most of our time. Rest allows us the opportunity to reflect, recharge, and refresh, which is pleasing to God because it honors the Biblical principle of godly rest. Without proper rest we're not able to work or serve at our best capacity. We lose interest more quickly and are unable to contribute creative ideas. We're not as focused, driven, or even interested in the task at hand.

Rest is not just sleeping, or a vacation or a getaway. Rest is self-care—an activity you engage in to pour into you and to regain your focus and strength. Rest can be a brisk morning walk, a midday massage, or a soothing bath before turning in for the night. However you choose to rest, make it an intentional part of your daily life rather than a periodical reward. Rest is not the cherry on top, it's a key component to your mental, spiritual and physical health.

In addition to physical rest, spiritual rest is essential as a daughter of God. God wants us to rest in His presence, allowing His spirit to refill us in ways nothing and no one else can. He wants to be our refuge, a soft place to land after we've invested our time, gifts and talents into fulfilling our purpose. God rested. Jesus rested. Let us, then, delight not only in our productivity but in the peace that comes from allowing God to fill us back up again.

So be ambitious. Go after your dreams. Work hard to achieve your goals, but in your quest for success, remember that it is God who truly satisfies you, not your accomplishments. In His infinite ability and lack of need for sleep or slumber, we can take refuge. We can take rest.

Reflect and Pray

I surrender the pressure to work hard and neglect rest. I choose rest—physical and spiritual—because it is a necessary piece of a productive life.

Lord, thank You that rest is pleasing to You. Help me to prioritize rest in my daily life as I pursue the dreams and goals You've placed in my heart.

In Jesus' name, Amen.

Choose Surrender

Therefore humble yourselves under the mighty hand of God [set aside self-righteous pride], so that He may exalt you [to a place of honor in His service] at the appropriate time.

1 Peter 5:6, AMP

Are you willing to put it all on the line for God?

It's a big question to ask yourself, but that's all surrender is—putting everything on the line and trusting God's direction over your own.

Whether you realize it or not, every devotional in this section has been about surrender, which is why we've ended each section with a reflection on surrendering something to God so you can choose His way instead. Choosing God always requires surrender because we can't obey His will and ours at the same time. We can't follow His tenets and the world's. We can't be in control while also letting Him guide us. In giving Him our surrender, we're giving Him total access and ability, which means He has the first and final say over our actions.

There is, perhaps, no harder choice for a daughter of God than surrender: The act of giving up whatever it is that you want in order to do what God wants. While we know that what God determines for us is always better than anything we could plan, choose, or create for ourselves, surrender still requires a radical denying of self that sometimes feels like betraying our own needs and wants for the will of God, which we often don't even know or understand.

Surrender is particularly hard when it doesn't directly serve us. For example, serving on a team at church requires you to follow the leader, having to surrender the way you would do things, and executing their directions when you feel like your ideas are better. Our flesh is stubborn and we don't always want to control it but a life of surrender to God will always yield the best fruit.

In the Garden of Gethsemane, Jesus gives us the ultimate example of surrender when He prays asking the Lord to keep Him from having to suffer His impending death on the cross. Even in His request, He ends with surrender: "And going a little farther, he fell on the ground and prayed that, if it were possible, the hour might pass from him. And he said, "Abba, Father, all things are possible for you. Remove this cup from me. Yet not what I will, but what you will" (Mark 14: 35-36, ESV).

Jesus knew He was literally born to die for us, yet He still had to bring His flesh to the point of acceptance. That's what true surrender is: acceptance. It's bringing your heart, mind, body, and spirit to a place of agreement: "Whatever you're asking, Lord, my soul says, *yes*."

Yes, when I'm broken. Yes, when I'm defeated. Yes, when I don't understand. Yes, when I benefit. Yes, when I suffer.

The greatest offering you'll ever give to God is your yes. And that yes comes at a cost. With or without God, we will have difficulty. When we choose surrender, we have a promise: this world cannot consume us. In John 16:33, Jesus said to His disciples, "I have said these things to you, that in me you may have peace. In the world you will have tribulation. But take heart; I have overcome the world" (ESV).

So the question remains, are you willing to put it all on the line for God? He's not asking you to do something He didn't already do for you while you were yet a sinner. You were, and still are, worth it.

So is He.

Reflect and Pray

I surrender my way, my plans, and my desires. I choose to follow Christ.

Lord, thank You for Your infinite wisdom, knowledge and power. Thank You that You see and know all things. Help me to submit and surrender myself to Your perfect will for my life and to trust that You will not fail me.

In Jesus' name, Amen.

Choose Wisdom

Joyful is the person who finds wisdom, the one who gains understanding. For wisdom is more profitable than silver, and her wages are better than gold. Wisdom is more precious than rubies; nothing you desire can compare with her. She offers you long life in her right hand, and riches and honor in her left. She will guide you down delightful paths; all her ways are satisfying. Wisdom is a tree of life to those who embrace her; happy are those who hold her tightly.

Proverbs 3: 13-18, NLT

This powerful passage in Proverbs shows the power of having wisdom, an undervalued quality that shifts the way we approach situations, decisions and relationships.

Wisdom means having good judgment and oftentimes, wisdom comes from experience, but experience is not the only way to get wisdom. Wisdom is a gift from God, and He will gladly give it to you if you ask for it. In 1 Kings 3 (NLT), the Lord appeared to Solomon in a dream and said, ""What do you want? Ask, and I will give it to you!" (v. 5). Solomon could've asked for anything in the world but he asked for wisdom, and it so greatly pleased the Lord that He blessed Solomon with wisdom *and* riches: "Because you have asked for wisdom in governing my people with justice and have not asked for a long life or wealth or the death of your enemies—I will give you what you asked for! I will give you a wise and understanding heart such as no one else has had or ever will have! And I will also give you what you did not ask for— riches and fame! No other king in all the world will be compared to you for the rest of your life!" (v. 11-13).

Wisdom is better than mere money because when you have wisdom, you'll know both how to earn money *and* how to properly manage it. Wisdom is better than mere opportunities because with wisdom you'll know how to seek, secure and steward the opportunities you receive. When you have wisdom, you will know how to approach any situation. You will have the foresight and insight to enter any season of your life with the confidence that despite lack of experience, you have the means to excel through the power and leading of the Lord.

Wisdom also comes from sitting with and gleaning from individuals who God places in your life to help guide you—parents, parental figures, pastors, mentors, etc. When the Lord blesses us with these relationships He affords us the opportunity for accelerated growth. Godly leaders will cover you in prayer, speak life into you, and warn you of trouble up ahead. When God gives you such a gift, always appreciate and honor the place this person holds in your life but be careful not to value that person's voice more than the Lord's.

Make sure your personal relationship with God is the first priority in your life so you can know for yourself what He wants you to do. Seeking the advice of others should be a secondary avenue for confirmation and support should the Lord lead you to inquire. If any advice the person gives you is in conflict with what God told you, don't hesitate to do what God told you to do.

Wisdom is vital because without it, you leave yourself more vulnerable to the enemy's attacks, and to being taken advantage of by people who don't have your best interest in mind. Through spending time in God's word and with God in prayer, we will gain the wisdom we need to lead fulfilling lives in Him.

You don't have to go through life making the best choices you can and hoping for the best. You have access to the wisdom it takes to step out on faith and know that the outcome is victory. In your daily prayer time, seek the Lord for wisdom in governing your life and the wisdom to make right decisions.

Reflect and Pray

I surrender the tendency to rely only on myself or others for direction. I choose to seek the Lord for the wisdom to make right and godly decisions.

Lord, thank You that I have access to wisdom. I ask that You bless me with the wisdom for what to do, how to do it, and when to do it. Help me to make wise decisions that please You and bring glory to Your name.

In Jesus' name, Amen.

Choose Worship

But the hour is coming, and now is, when the true worshipers will worship the
Father in spirit and truth; for the Father is seeking such to worship Him.
God is Spirit, and those who worship Him must worship in spirit and truth."

John 4:23-24, NKJV

When you think of worship, what comes to mind? Maybe it's your favorite worship song or hymn, the song you kept on replay during the loneliest season of your life, or your go-to playlist during your prayer time.

While worship can be accompanied by music, it's not defined by it. Worship is simply the act of expressing your love to God in the way that feels most authentic to you—singing, speaking in tongues, lifting your hands, kneeling down or stretching out, crying, etc. However you express your worship to God, what matters is that your worship is honest and true.

Worship is glorifying God, not just for the things He's done for you, but for who He is to you. When we think about who God's been to us, worship should be our natural response. God is our provider, protector, keeper, and sustainer. He is loving, loyal and consistent. He is our friend. Our help. Our hope. He is a good, *good* Father who deserves our adoration.

Worship should be a daily act for a daughter of God because every day God is worthy. Every time you think of something God's done for you, make it a habit to whisper a word of thanks. In Psalm 103:1-5, David said, "Bless the Lord, O my soul; and all that is within me, bless His holy name! Bless the Lord, O my soul, and forget not all His benefits: who forgives all your iniquities, who heals all your diseases, who redeems your life from destruction, who crowns you with lovingkindness and tender mercies, who satisfies your mouth with good things, so that your youth is renewed like the eagle's" (Version). Worship requires reflection—reminding ourselves of all the times God came through for us and coming back, once again, to say,

"Thank you." When we fully immerse ourselves in retrospection of just how good, kind, and faithful God has been to us, gratitude flows from our hearts to His feet. *That* is worship.

It costs us nothing to worship when God's favor is evident in our lives, but you have to really love and trust God to worship Him when you're hurting—after a disappointing no, during a breakup or divorce, upon receiving news that you've lost a loved one. During these times of turmoil, distress, and defeat, worship may feel like the last thing you want to do. It's also the only thing that will get you *through*. Even in the thick of trouble, we owe God a sacrifice of praise, an offering that says, "You're still God. You're still good."

The same God who blesses also comforts. The same God who provides also preserves. The same God who anoints your head with oil is the one who sustains you in times of suffering. No emotion we feel is foreign or offensive to Him. We can bring Him our questions, our confusion, our sadness, our emptiness, and in return receive understanding, peace, joy, and fulfillment. His love makes us whole.

When we worship God in every season of our lives we will experience the keeping power of God that carries us through both our trials and our victories. In all things, He is good. In all things, He is worthy.

Reflect and Pray

I surrender everything I'm going through right now. I choose to give God my worship, even when I walk through difficult seasons.

Lord, You alone are worthy of my worship. Help me to bless Your holy name no matter what circumstance I'm currently in. I trust that You are in control and that Your presence satisfies and completes me. Fill my cup, Lord.

In Jesus' name, Amen.

Choose The New You

Not that I have already obtained it [this goal of being Christlike] or have already been made perfect, but I actively press on so that I may take hold of that [perfection] for which Christ Jesus took hold of me and made me His own. Brothers and sisters, I do not consider that I have made it my own yet; but one thing I do: forgetting what lies behind and reaching forward to what lies ahead, I press on toward the goal to win the [heavenly] prize of the upward call of God in Christ Jesus.

Philippians 3:12-14, AMP

Have you ever felt like your past was holding you hostage?

Throughout this section we've focused on choosing what's right—those characteristics that create a life that pleases and honors God, but the greatest thing that threatens your progress is *your past*.

The enemy will always try to use your past against you because he knows that everything God has in store for you is ahead of you, not behind you. He wants you to dwell on your past mistakes, what you could've done better or differently, and the areas of your life that didn't pan out the way you would've hoped. He wants you to dwell on the ifs: *If I hadn't gotten into that relationship, I would've been married by now. If I had gone to college I would be making more money by now. If I hadn't made that decision, I would have the life I wanted by now.*

There's no value or power in hypothesizing what your life would be if you hadn't chosen, gone through, or experienced what you did. There is power in confronting your past, accepting the truth of what happened, and choosing where you will go from here.

We cannot walk boldly into our future and become who God called us to be with the weight of our past dragging us down. For this reason, it's important to face trauma, disappointment, and grief head-on. We can't avoid our past and we can't get around having to mourn not only what happened, but what *didn't* happen. It's time to mourn what trauma stole from you so that when you receive this next blessing, you'll be able to celebrate without the pain of regret or the negative memory of what you lost.

Just like a butterfly has to break through her cocoon to fully become this new version of herself, you have to break free of the shell you've been in. That shell allowed you the time and room you needed to grow and to heal, but now it's time to fully step into your newness. It's time to leave the old you behind. It's time to soar.

You are *not* what happened to you. No longer will you define your life by where you fell short. Grace is your portion. As you allow the mercy and love of God to overshadow yesterday's disappointments, a bright, new day is waiting for the new you to appear, the new you that's been cultivated throughout the progression of this devotional. Know that as you embrace this next, new season of your life, God is removing the reminder of what *was*. He's erasing the residue that your past cast on you. He's giving you new opportunities to create memories you will think fondly upon rather than avoid.

So much awaits the free, healed, and whole you. That home, that possession, the new job, the healthy marriage, the growing family, and everything else you're believing God for are waiting. It's time for the dreams you've had in your heart for years to become your reality. Destiny is calling and your time is now here.

You made it, girl. Welcome to the other side.

Reflect and Pray

I surrender every negative thought and experience from my past. I choose to embrace the new me and step into my future with the bold confidence that what's coming is better than what's been.

Lord, thank You for bringing me this far. Thank You for never leaving nor forsaking me. Even at my lowest moments, You were there. Thank You that my past cannot hold me or stop me from enjoying a full life in You. Thank You that I made it to the end of a long journey back to myself—the person You created and called me to be. I'm ready for what's next.

In Jesus' name, Amen.

WHATEVER IS PURE

Release the old. Pursue the new.

Now that you've rediscovered who God says you are, have worked to become more like Jesus, and have surrendered your way for His, it's time to approach your life in Christ with a fresh start. The Word of God says "This means that anyone who belongs to Christ has become a new person. The old life is gone; a new life has begun!" (2 Corinthians 5:17, NLT).

Up until this point, your life has been marked by the decisions you made and the things that happened to you but now the Lord is wiping the slate clean and giving you a renewed opportunity to create and pursue a life of holiness, a life that honors Him. No matter what you've done or where you've been, this bold, new life is available to you.

Something that is pure is free of sin and/or free of the damaging effects of sin. Romans 6:23 says, "For the wages of sin is death; but the gift of God is eternal life through Jesus Christ our Lord" (NLT). The payment for our wrongdoings is death, but because Jesus went to the cross and bore the shame and responsibility of our sin, we are free and can offer our lives as a living sacrifice, holy and acceptable to the Lord, the only appropriate response to such a gift. (Romans 12:1).

You've suffered. You've endured. You've persevered. You've evolved. Now it's time to pursue. As you pursue the things of God, there will be some things you have to release in order to experience the life God has planned for you. As you embark on the last leg of this journey, remember that you are a miracle. A generational curse breaker. One of one. When you pursue what God has for you, you will discover just how much He truly satisfies those who seek after Him. You will not be disappointed, but amazed. Bewildered. Overjoyed. In *awe*. God loves you *that* much. And it's time for your whole life to become evidence of that love.

Pursue Purpose

You are the salt of the earth, but if salt has lost its taste, how shall its saltiness be restored? It is no longer good for anything except to be thrown out and trampled under people's feet. You are the light of the world. A city set on a hill cannot be hidden. Nor do people light a lamp and put it under a basket, but on a stand, and it gives light to all in the house. In the same way, let your light shine before others, so that they may see your good works and give glory to your Father who is in heaven.

Matthew 5:13-16, ESV

There's nothing more fulfilling than pursuing God's purpose for your life.

Satan knows this, and he makes it his business to try to keep you from fulfilling your God-given purpose.

Maybe you've been running from your purpose because you don't feel worthy of it. Maybe you don't know what your purpose is, or maybe you're afraid to fully throw yourself into purpose because you don't feel secure that God will provide. Wherever you find yourself, rest assured that God wants to use you and that He *will* take care of you.

Your ultimate purpose is to bring glory to God and to be a light that draws others to Him. How you go about doing that is your calling. What you're called to will be different in different seasons of your life because God created us to be ever-changing and ever-developing. That's the beauty of living a full life in God: we are multifaceted and don't have to be tied down to one career or passion for the rest of our lives. In one season of your life, you may be called to be a teacher. In another season, a hairstylist. In another, the owner of your own shop. *How* you execute your purpose changes, but as what you're called to shifts throughout your life, never lose sight of *why* you do what you do—your purpose.

Pursuing purpose is exciting, especially when you're first starting out. At times, pursuing purpose will be taxing. Draining. Scary. Intense. Again, that's because the enemy knows that you fulfilling your purpose in God is a massive threat to his agenda to kill, steal, and destroy. You don't have to fear the enemy's attacks when you fix your eyes on God and keep your focus on what He's called you to do.

Purpose isn't something you have to chase or discover. By doing what God called you to do with the gifts He's given you to use for the people He's assigned you to reach, you are pursuing purpose. As you execute your purpose, God will provide you with everything you need to live and give you the ability to earn wealth. In surrendering your life to God and using your gifts to build His kingdom, there's no good thing that God will withhold from you.

He will give you ideas and strategies. He will guide your steps. He will help you to properly steward what He's blessed you with so you never have to lack, worry or struggle. Matthew 6:31-33 (NLT) says, "So don't worry about these things, saying, 'What will we eat? What will we drink? What will we wear?' These things dominate the thoughts of unbelievers, but your heavenly Father already knows all your needs. Seek the Kingdom of God above all else, and live righteously, and he will give you everything you need."

Whenever you feel as though you're getting off track or losing your way, take a moment to put things back in perspective. Remind yourself of *why* you do what you do. Remind yourself of *Who* you do it for. Fix your eyes back on God. Let Him get the glory out of your life.

Reflect and Pray

I release any worry I have associated with pursuing the purpose God for me. I will boldly pursue God's purpose for my life with the assurance that He will take care of me because He always provides.

Lord, thank You for the purpose You've given me to spread the Good News and be a light by which others can see You. Thank You for taking care of me and everything that concerns me as I endeavor to execute my purpose. I trust that You are in control and that You will help me do what pleases You.

In Jesus' name, Amen.

Pursue Relationship

Behold, I stand at the door and knock. If anyone hears my voice and opens the door, I will come in to him and eat with him, and he with me.

Revelation 3:20, ESV

There's nothing more fulfilling than enjoying a close and personal relationship with God.

Sermons, Christian podcasts and devotionals are all valuable additions to our walk with God, but none of these external resources can or should substitute quality time spent with God through prayer, worship, and reading your Bible for yourself.

God knows you better than you know yourself, and He wants you to get to know Him deeply. There are revelations God wants to speak to you directly, words of encouragement He wants to pour into your spirit, and directions He wants you to take. Receiving God-given prophecies is wonderful as it gives us confirmation regarding what God is going to do in our lives. God doesn't want you to rely on prophecies to know what He wants you to do. God wants to speak *to you*, and for Him to do that you must be in a place to hear Him. The more time you spend getting to know and understand God, the more you'll be able to identify His voice. He will speak to you directly but He also speaks through dreams, songs, and visions. Be sensitive to His spirit and open to however God wants to show up.

Beyond what you've heard in church or on social media, God wants you to know Him intimately. When Jesus died for our sins, we gained direct access to God. We don't need a high priest to enter God's presence on our behalf. We can experience God's presence for ourselves anytime, anywhere. When you know God for yourself, the enemy can't use lies to deter you from becoming who God created you to be.

God longs to pour into you and give you power, wisdom, and clarity. When you provide God access to every detail of your life, His unmerited favor will give you a unique advantage. You'll start receiving opportunities you couldn't have gotten in your own strength or ability, all because you were sensitive to the voice of the Lord. Don't hesitate to welcome God's presence into every atmosphere you occupy—not just at home or at church, but at work, in your car, in the grocery store, etc. When you give God access, He will upgrade every part of your life.

God wants to hear from you and He wants to speak to you. He wants you to enjoy the abundant life that living in His presence provides. Even now, He stands at the door and knocks, hoping that You will let Him in to dine with you. Don't leave Him waiting.

Reflect and Pray

I release the tendency to let other things take priority over pursuing my personal relationship with God. I will delight in His presence and pursue my own, personal relationship with Him.

Lord, thank You for opening my eyes to the importance of having my own relationship with You. Forgive me for every time I didn't prioritize my personal connection with You. Help me to put You first so that I can enjoy a full, abundant life in Your presence.

In Jesus' name, Amen.

Pursue Righteousness

Blessed are those who hunger and thirst for righteousness,
for they shall be satisfied.

Matthew 5:6, ESV

Righteousness is not about perfection, but a lifelong pursuit. You won't get it right all the time, but when you pursue righteousness, you're making a conscious decision to discount your old, sinful nature and adopt the character of Jesus.

Romans 12:2 says, "And do not be conformed to this world, but be transformed by the renewing of your mind, that you may prove what is that good and acceptable and perfect will of God" (NKJV). Our natural, human inclination is to sin. It takes the power of the Holy Spirit to control our flesh and train ourselves to behave in a way that honors God. Before righteousness is ever an external expression, it is first a posture of the heart.

Because you are a daughter of God, it's important to hold up a certain standard that sets you apart from others. People should be able to recognize your stance. Even without opening your mouth and declaring that you're a Christian, people should notice that there's something different about you. They shouldn't feel comfortable acting any kind of way around you. Instead, they should feel convicted by the anointing of God that rests on your life.

Too many people want to blend in, worried that they'll miss out on opportunities or offend others if they're too vocal about their faith in God. God is looking for women who will boldly declare their faith and are willing to speak out about who God is and what He's done for them. When you pursue righteousness, you aren't worried about what people think about you but you're concerned with living holy so others can witness that Christ dwells on the inside of you. It is the Spirit of God that enables us to live a righteous life in Him. We can't do it on our own.

Note that there's a difference between being righteous and being *self-righteous*. When you're self-righteous, you base your value in the Kingdom upon the good deeds you've done, looking down on others and placing yourself on a pedestal because you don't engage in certain actions or behaviors.

We should be careful not to adopt this arrogant attitude because it's a form of pride that is offensive to God and a poor reflection of His nature. No matter how "good" we think we are, we are never without need of the grace, mercy, and forgiveness of God. Be careful not to forget that it is not our good deeds that save us, but the grace of God: "For by grace you have been saved through faith. And this is not your own doing; it is the gift of God, not a result of works, so that no one may boast" (Ephesians 2:8-9, ESV). Our good deeds don't make us righteous—only the Lord can do that.

As you seek to honor the Lord in your actions and decisions, remember that He's the one who makes you righteous. It is by no goodness of your own that you are saved, that you are holy, and that you are His.

Reflect and Pray

I release self-righteous behaviors and attempting to be righteous in my own strength. As I pursue righteousness, I recognize that it is only through the power and grace of God that I'm able to please Him.

Lord, thank You for Your grace and mercy that covers and keeps me. Thank You for making me righteous as I endeavor to be more like You. Lord, let others see You in me.

In Jesus name, Amen.

Pursue His Promises

For as many as are the promises of God, in Christ they are [all answered] "Yes."
So through Him we say our "Amen" to the glory of God.

2 Corinthians 1:20, AMP

If someone's ever made a promise to you and broken it, you know the utter disappointment and frustration that comes from banking on what someone said and coming up short. Enduring your fair share of broken promises can make you jaded, uninterested in believing or hoping again because you've been let down time and time again.

The good news is, God never breaks a promise. In fact, He goes above and beyond to fulfill His promise to you in the time He destined for it to happen. While God's promises take time to come to fruition, we can always be sure that they will come to pass.

The question is not whether God will do it, because He will. The question is, are you willing to wait until He does? Without patience, we may find ourselves attempting to "play God" in our lives, exhausting our means trying to fulfill a promise He made us when we don't have the ability or understanding to see it through. We don't know what God is doing behind the scenes. We don't know what He's orchestrating or how He's clearing the path for our blessing to reach us. We don't know all that needs to happen before our promise can meet us.

All we can and should do is trust that God has not forgotten, remain ready for the next instruction, and be prepared to move at the moment He gives us the green light. We will never know everything, but He always gives us enough knowledge to make the next step.

God's promises require preparation, and sometimes the waiting period we're in is to prepare us for the blessing. It is not God's intention to bless you with something you're not ready to receive because any blessing without the proper timing and preparation can easily become a curse. God wants you to have the home of your dreams but first, He wants you to clean up your finances. God wants you to have a kingdom marriage but first, He wants you to go to therapy. God isn't trying to keep any of His blessings from you. He's trying to keep *you* from fumbling them. He loves you too much to let you wait this long only to lose the blessing as soon as you get it.

If you're in a season of waiting, know that there's purpose in the waiting. Don't wait idly, angry with God that He hasn't yet given you the desires of your heart. Consider what the waiting is teaching you and in every circumstance, find yourself content. Rather than wasting your time sulking, spend it praising God in advance for what He's getting ready to do for you. He will impress you with the magnitude of His love for you. He will fill your life with beautiful things.

Do you trust that the Lord will keep His promise to you? Are you willing to wait on Him to come through? The journey to your promise coming to pass may feel long and arduous, but in the end it will all be worth it. Hold on and wait just a little while longer. God always comes through.

Reflect and Pray

I release any unbelief I've attached to the promise God made me. In pursuing the promises of God, I'm willing to obey His instructions. I'm willing to wait.

Lord, thank You that all Your promises are yes and amen. I trust that You will keep every promise that You've made to me. Help me to keep the faith as I wait for the promise to come to pass. Help me to patiently obey Your instructions with confidence that You will do just what You said.

In Jesus' name, Amen.

Pursue Healing

Beloved, I pray that in every way you may succeed and prosper and be in good health [physically], just as [I know] your soul prospers [spiritually].

3 John 1:2, AMP

"I just want to be free."

After embarking on my healing journey, I said these words to God so many times—usually after He'd revealed to me some hurt, some pain, some unhealthy habit that was still lurking in my heart. But one particular time when I said those words, the Lord replied to me, "You are free. Now it's time to heal."

Freedom is often a moment but healing is *always* a process. We see people get touched and delivered from demons and illnesses, but we don't see the *after*. Having to go home and face the person in the mirror and how you got to the point of even needing deliverance in the first place. Having to go to therapy to understand yourself and why you do the things you do. Having to break habits you've been comfortable with for years in exchange for healthy ones that feel foreign to you because dysfunction is all you've ever known. Having to break ties with people you no longer have anything in common with and cut off friends who mean you no good. Having to say no to things that may not convict others because God's calling you to a higher level of accountability. Healing is *messy.* We have to be committed to the process of our healing if we want to maintain the freedom God gave us.

Pursuing healing means being committed to the process. God loves you so much that He is patient with you in the process because He knows how much you can handle. He knows at what point He can peel back another layer where healing needs to take place. He won't overwhelm you to the point that you can't bear the pressure of facing what lies beneath the surface, but He will gently nudge you towards change.

No matter how ugly or difficult it may be to face the rejection, loneliness, abandonment, desperation, or other emotion that led you to make the decisions you made, or to voice offenses the old you would have silenced, it's worth the work. Healing is not a onetime thing; it comes in waves.

As you're pursuing purpose, healing becomes inevitable because those unhealed places will hinder you from thriving in purpose. When you're on the verge of fulfilling an assignment God gave you or receiving a blessing God promised you, it seems everything you still need to heal from comes out of the woodwork. While confronting those emotions is painful, it's better to deal with them now than to drag trauma into your promised land.

You owe it to yourself to go all in with your healing process. If it takes staying in therapy for a year, do it. If it means taking some time away from social media, do it. If God puts it on your heart to go on a fast, do it. Whatever you do, don't rush your process. Don't sugarcoat it. Let it be messy. Let it be ugly. Let it be complete.

Reflect and Pray

I release everything that's blocking me from total healing. As I pursue healing, I won't rush it. I welcome the process because I'm worth the outcome.

Father, thank You that You're healing me from the inside out. I believe that You will do a complete work in me so that I can serve You at my greatest capacity. Help me to remain faithful to the process despite what is unearthed in me along the way.

In Jesus' name, Amen.

Pursue Life

The thief does not come except to steal, and to kill, and to destroy. I have come that they may have life, and that they may have it more abundantly.

John 10:10, NKJV

"I want you to *live*."

God spoke these words to me on a day that completely altered the trajectory of my life. Up until that point, I'd been living a life that was beneath what God had planned and promised me. From that moment forward, I slowly started progressing toward reclaiming who I was and the life God always wanted me to have.

The life that God has for us is one of joy, peace, abundance and fulfillment. God doesn't want us to be broke, depressed, anxious, stressed, confused, or lonely. While we sometimes experience those things, it's not God's will for us to remain there, which is why He always provides a way of escape from life's burdens. God wants you whole. God wants you *well*.

The enemy doesn't want you to experience the abundant life God has in mind for you. From the moment you were born he's been plotting and scheming to disrupt God's purpose for your life. He knows what a force to be reckoned with you will be if you overcome the obstacles he's placed in your path so he tries to chip away at your confidence and your resolve. He orchestrates generational curses and sets up traps for you to fall into so you never fully realize who you are and what you're capable of. He sends negative thoughts and spiritual attacks your way to discourage you from living for God so you never reach the souls God's assigned to you.

It's true, being a daughter of God will come with its fair share of challenges. You will suffer. You will go through hardships. You will experience disappointment and pain. God's word promises us that despite being tried, we will not be destroyed: "We are hard-pressed on every side, yet not crushed; we are perplexed, but not in despair; persecuted, but not forsaken; struck down, but not destroyed" (2 Corinthians 4:8-9, NKJV).

In God, you have so much to live for and look forward to. You were created on purpose and for purpose. God is *not* finished with you and He's not done fulfilling His promises to you. Don't give up on God. Don't give up on you. Keep going, keep pushing, keep praying and believing. Your abundant life awaits.

Reflect and Pray

I release the discouragement that's stopping me from fully owning my purpose. I'm pursuing the life God has for me without hesitation or fear of what's up the road.

Lord, thank You that in You, I have access to an abundant life. Help me to take my focus off what the enemy is attempting to do and instead, focus on You and what You've promised me. I'm reclaiming the life You promised me.

In Jesus' name, Amen.

Pursue Peace

"I am leaving you with a gift—peace of mind and heart. And the peace I give is a gift the world cannot give. So don't be troubled or afraid.

John 14:27, NLT

Everywhere you turn, it seems as though there's a threat to your peace. From the person in the vehicle that cut you off on your way home to the co-worker who makes it their business to work the last nerve you have, every day we're presented with challenges that will thwart our peace if we aren't intentional about protecting it.

When inconveniences come to disrupt your peace, it can be a real fight to maintain your calm and keep a level head. Perspective changes everything, and when we learn not to take circumstances at face value and instead, understand what the enemy is attempting to do, we can avoid losing our peace.

The enemy knows what a gift it is to have the peace of God. He knows that the peace of God surpasses all understanding. It doesn't make sense to have a smile on your face knowing that your mom is battling cancer. It doesn't make sense to be stress-free when you have 67 cents to your name. It is only when you have God's peace that you can see *past* your situation and hold onto your hope. You can see your loved one on the other side of this, completely healed. You can say, "This too, shall pass," and mean it.

God doesn't want your circumstances to consume you. That is why 1 Peter 5:7 (NLT) encourages you to "give all your worries and cares to God, for he cares about you." When you give it over to God, your situation might not change instantaneously. What will change is your perspective; your perspective creates your reality.

No matter what's on your plate today, you can give it to God in exchange for His peace. Once you've put your problem in His hands, resist the urge to take it back. Every time it crosses your mind, utter a word of thanks unto God instead of a complaint.

Reflect and Pray

I release the worry that's plaguing my thoughts and preventing me from resting at night. I'm pursuing peace by casting my cares upon the Lord and allowing Him to be my strength.

Lord, thank You that You are interested, concerned with and moved by everything that distresses me. As I give You my issue, thank You for lifting the worry and allowing me to rest in Your safety, protection, and peace.

In Jesus' name, Amen.

Pursue Community

As iron sharpens iron, so a friend sharpens a friend.

Proverbs 27:17, NLT

You weren't created to do life alone, and the enemy knows this. He wants you to isolate yourself because when you don't have anyone praying for you or helping to keep you accountable, you become more susceptible to the enemy's tactics. In godly community, there is safety and protection.

Sometimes our reluctance to pursue and appreciate community stems from rejection. When you've made yourself vulnerable to community in the past and been wounded, it's hard to let your guard down again. God wants you to be in godly community with other believers because it provides a greater opportunity for you to advance in the Kingdom. God will put you alongside individuals who will see the best in you and help pull out the greatness God's placed inside of you. In godly community there is no jealousy or competition, there is only love and support as you push one another to go after the things of God.

In community, it's important to communicate your boundaries because doing so keeps you from compromising your capacity. No matter how hard you try, you can't show up for everything. If you aren't able or don't want to do something, don't be afraid to communicate that to your friend. A person who genuinely loves and respects you will also respect your boundaries. They won't want you to commit to tasks when you don't have the time or resources to follow through.

Community is not about control, and anytime you're experiencing control within a community, it's a red flag. No one should be attempting to control or manipulate you into doing what they want you to do. If you find yourself in a situation that feels restrictive or unsafe, don't feel obligated to stay. God wants you in a healthy community where you are able to be honest and free to be yourself.

Ask God to give you a community you can count on that will encourage you, help you, show up for you, and offer you a safe space to grow and heal.

Reflect and Pray

I release the hurt and rejection I've experienced from people in the past. No longer will I those negative experiences keep me from pursuing community.

Lord, thank You for creating us to be in community with one another. Put the right people in my life to encourage me and help me thrive in the purpose You created me for.

In Jesus' name, Amen.

Pursue Service

Each of you should use whatever gift you have received to serve others, as faithful stewards of God's grace in its various forms. If anyone speaks, they should do so as one who speaks the very words of God. If anyone serves, they should do so with the strength God provides, so that in all things God may be praised through Jesus Christ. To him be the glory and the power for ever and ever. Amen.

1 Peter 4:10-11, NIV

Even though we were put on Earth to serve others, it doesn't always come naturally. As long as we live in this flesh, we will have to work to resist and overcome our sinful nature. It is in our nature to do what we feel like serves our interests, not what will benefit others.

Some people have the spiritual gift of helping, which makes them naturally more inclined to serve others any way they can because this is the way they show love. Some people go out of their way to do for others because they have a deep desire to belong. They long to be loved, accepted, and feel that serving others will fill that void. On the surface, it may appear as though they're selfless but really they serve out of fear of not being loved or needed.

As you pursue service, make sure it isn't because you're trying to prove that you're worthy of love and acceptance, but because you genuinely want to help others. Remember that your worth comes from God, not the good deeds that you do, and you are already loved and accepted by God.

It pleases God when we serve others because "even the Son of Man came not to be served but to serve others and to give his life as a ransom for many" (Matthew 20:28, NLT). True love is sacrificial. If you're not willing to give, you're not willing to love. As you go about your day-to-day activities, look for ways that you can help someone else so that the love of God can flow through you.

Ultimately, we can never make a greater sacrifice than Jesus has already done for us. If we serve others in a way that shows even a fraction of the love He bestowed upon us, we'll be on the right track.

Reflect and Pray

I release the natural, selfish tendency to look out only for myself and those that are close to me. In my daily life, I will look for opportunities to serve others.

Lord, thank You for creating me to serve others. Help me find ways to give my time, gifts, talents and resources to better the lives of others.

In Jesus' name, Amen.

Pursue Diligently

Lazy people want much but get little, while the diligent are prospering.

Proverbs 13:4, TLB

To be diligent is to continuously put forth effort in order to achieve something. A diligent person doesn't give up at the first sign of struggle; instead, they find a way around or plow their way through to get the job done. God has endless blessings lined up for you, but you won't receive them all if you're resistant to the work it takes to seize them.

We're quick to say we want something. We're slow to take continuous action towards obtaining it. You want a thriving business but you have yet to invest in a coaching program or mentorship to help you create one. You want to level up in your career but you have yet to build the connections necessary to progress. God isn't withholding anything from you; what you desire is well within reach if you'll put action behind your words.

No one wants to be called lazy, but we have to face the harsh reality that when we're unwilling to put forth the effort it takes to accomplish great things, that's what we are: lazy. In addition to a disinterest in working hard, what many people lack is stickability—the staying power it takes to remain faithful when you aren't seeing the desired results. It may take weeks, months, years to possess the promise, but you'll never even get a glimpse of it if you quit in the middle. Some people don't know what it feels like to experience a hard-won victory because they've never not given up.

In order to persevere, you have to learn how to encourage yourself. If you're always depending on someone else to pat you on the back, you won't get very far. When you master the art of digging deep and pressing in, you'll be able to accomplish more than even you thought you had in you.

There's more in you than what you're used to settling for. You know what it's like when you're running out of toothpaste so you roll it up to squeeze that last little bit of toothpaste out of the tube. You just needed enough for one day but you discover that you have enough to last another week. And that's because there's more than what naturally comes to the surface, but you have to dig for it. You have to *press*.

This season will require tenacity. Force. Determination. This time when you apply pressure, don't retreat. Go full speed ahead and you will be surprised by what you accomplish.

Reflect and Pray

I release the part of me that's unwilling to work hard for the things I want to happen for me. Instead of just talking about it, I'm willing to put action behind my words and diligently pursue everything I desire to obtain.

Lord, thank You for giving me the ability to diligently pursue my dreams with the assurance that You've already given me the power to persevere. Help me to stick to the plan so that I can prosper.

In Jesus' name, Amen.

Pursue Confidently

But blessed is the man who trusts in the Lord and has made the Lord his hope and confidence. He is like a tree planted along a riverbank, with its roots reaching deep into the water—a tree not bothered by the heat nor worried by long months of drought. Its leaves stay green, and it goes right on producing all its luscious fruit.

Jeremiah 117:7-8, TLB

Your lack of confidence is one of the greatest threats to your destiny. Confidence is the bold assurance that what you bring to the table is valuable and that you're the one for the task. When you're confident, you're not worried about how others perceive or receive you. Your only concern is with showing up and doing what God called you to do in the way He created you to do it. If you believe you don't have what it takes, that will become your reality. As you endeavor to pursue purpose and go after all God's called you to, take time to address the areas where you lack confidence in yourself, getting to the root of the issue so that you can face it head-on.

Without confidence you won't be eager to rise up and get things done. Because you're afraid the end result won't be good enough, you drag your feet instead of fight to finish. Sometimes your lack of confidence is really a perceived lack of worth—thinking that you're unworthy of the blessing, unworthy of the promise, unworthy of the life of your dreams because of what transpired in your past. Old things have passed away. You are good enough. You are smart enough. You are the one for this great task.

Sometimes we hesitate to fully own our confidence because we don't want people to think we're arrogant. But if you keep in perspective that everything you are and everything you have to offer is because of God's favor on your life, you don't have to worry about being arrogant instead of confident. When you're arrogant, you have misplaced the credit for what you've accomplished and you think more highly of yourself than you should. Even with you putting forth the effort to accomplish a task, it's still God who gives you the strength and ability to pursue it. He is the one who made you creative. He's the one who woke you up in the middle of the night and gave you the exact strategy to implement to land that contract or ace that exam. We can be confident in ourselves when we are confident *in Him*.

It's time to stop letting your lack of confidence stand in the way of who you can be. When you put your trust and confidence in God, you will produce like never before. Own your creativity. Own your uniqueness. Own what makes you *you*, and let God use it for His glory.

Reflect and Pray

I release every negative word and experience that has resulted in my lack of confidence. I will confidently pursue what God has for me with the assurance that He made me capable of succeeding.

Lord, thank You that as I set out to do everything You've called me to do, You are backing me up. Help me to believe in myself and the talents You've given me.

In Jesus' name, Amen.

Pursue Fearlessly

Have I not commanded you? Be strong and courageous. Do not be frightened,
and do not be dismayed, for the Lord your God is with you wherever you go.

Joshua 1:9, ESV

Because the enemy can't stop you from progressing forward, he attempts to get you to fear what's up ahead. He wants you to be afraid that you can't handle the magnitude of the blessing, or that because you're stepping into uncharted territory, you won't know what to do when you get there. In response to the enemy attempting to make you afraid of the unknown, you can be confident that nothing is unknown to the God you serve, the God whose daughter you are. He's already in tomorrow. He's equipping you today for what's to come.

Fear is a paralyzing sense of being overwhelmed and defeated in the face of trouble, danger, or uncertainty. If we don't fight fear by leveraging the word of God, we'll miss out on our promised land because we're too afraid to step in the direction of the blessing. It's okay to be afraid; it's a perfectly natural and human response to anything that feels like a threat to our comfort zone. It's not okay to let fear be louder than the voice of God or to let fear take the place of the word God gave you.

All throughout the Bible you can encounter examples of Biblical heroes who stood in the face of fear and won. Moses stood up to Pharaoh and led the Israelites out of Egypt. Elijah stood up to the prophets of Baal and won. Gideon stood up to the Midianites and defeated them. Esther risked her life by going to the king without an invitation in order to save her people. Just as God strengthened and encouraged them, He's doing the same for you. Even now, He's lifting you up out of that pit of doubt and setting you on a mountain that's built on your trust in Him. Anytime you feel insignificant or incapable, remind yourself that your help comes from the Lord. You don't have to fear when your trust is in His might and not your own.

The next time fear tries to block you from your destiny, attack it with the Word of God: "For God has not given us a spirit of fear, but of power and of love and of a sound mind" (2 Timothy 1:7, NKJV).

Reflect and Pray

I release the fear that's blocking me from stepping into my destiny. Going forward I will confront fear instead of running from it by speaking the word over that fear and trusting that God has me covered.

Lord, thank You for your Word that reminds me of who I am in You. Thank You that I don't have to fear tomorrow because You're already there. Help me to face every fear that arises as I pursue my purpose with the courage that You go with, before, and behind me, covering and protecting me from danger and distress.

In Jesus' name, Amen.

Pursue Relentlessly

Let us not become weary in doing good, for at the proper time we will reap a harvest if we do not give up.

Galatians 6:9, NIV

Sometimes we give up too easily.

Everything God has for you won't come easily. There are some blessings you're going to have to work for and you have to be willing to press in when you're tired, to keep fighting when you want to give up, and to keep believing in yourself when the odds are stacked against you. Never let a "no" from man cause you to question the "yes" you already received from God. Believe in yourself. Believe in the gifts and talents God's given you. Don't stop until what He showed you is yours.

God's promises require your investment just as much as your belief. God always does His part, but you have to be willing to yours by being an active participant in what you're believing God to do *through you*. "For as the body without the spirit is dead, so faith without works is dead also" (James 2:26, ESV). What you're believing God for in this season won't just "happen." His promises are yes and amen, but you have a key role to play. Investing in the promise looks like putting action behind your faith. If you're believing God for a record deal, you should have songs written and ready to record. If you're believing God for your own clothing line, you should be working on your designs and your business plan.

Investing in the promise will cost you time, effort, energy, and even money, but inaction won't get you to the promise. You have to take God-led action to obtain it. Don't say you're "waiting on God" when you're really just afraid to move or make a mistake. Get moving and allow God to order your steps. Believe in the dream He placed in your heart enough to pursue it relentlessly. Rather than focusing on resources you don't have, use what's in your hand and God will bless and multiply it.

Some blessings have a window of completion. I wrote the bulk of this devotional while pregnant and after giving birth to my son. There were many times when I felt I didn't have the grace and strength to finish, but I knew I had to finish it before the end of the year because that was the window of completion God gave me. If you find yourself in a place where you don't have the motivation or discipline to keep going, let me encourage you, as God encouraged me: no matter your circumstance, completion is still well within your realm of ability.

Stop looking at what you don't have and capitalize on what you do. It's your time, you just have to tap into the power that works in you and know that He will enable you to see it through to the end.

Aren't you ready to find out what will happen if you don't stop this time? Then get up every day and work toward the dream God placed in your heart. Set your focus. Make a plan. Trust that the same God who gave you the vision has also given you the grace to finish. Stay the course. Finish well.

Reflect and Pray

I release laziness, defeat, and every other mindset that's blocking me from finishing what I started. I will pursue relentlessly so I can obtain what God promised me.

Lord, thank You for the dream You've placed in my heart. Help me to pursue it without fear that I can't see it through. Thank You for giving me the strength, strategy, wisdom, and resources I need to achieve it.

In Jesus' name, Amen.

Pursue Ministry

For God is not unjust to forget your work and labor of love which you have shown toward His name, in that you have ministered to the saints, and do minister.

Hebrews 6:10, NKJV

When people think of ministry, they usually think of preaching and teaching the word of God, leading worship, or serving within the church in some capacity. Ministry isn't just what you do within the four walls of the church, it's what you do when you serve others using the gifts, time, and resources God's given you: at work, at school, in business, etc., so that others can encounter the love of Jesus through you. If we limit ministry to within the church, we'll miss out on the countless opportunities to share the redeeming message of Jesus Christ with others through our everyday, ordinary experiences.

If you're going to pursue ministry, it's best to be passionate about it, which means your heart has to be in it. When you're not passionate about ministry, it's easy to fall into the traps of performance and obligation—either doing it because you're good at it or because it's expected of you, and neither is pleasing to God. To work in ministry, your heart's desire should be being God's vessel. With that posture you'll take your work seriously because you're doing it unto the Lord.

When it comes to ministry, you have to be all in. Otherwise, you won't fully invest in what God's entrusted you with. And God is looking for daughters who are willing to give God everything they have—their time, their resources, their gifts—and let God multiply it. God desires to raise up daughters who are serious about their calling and whom He can trust with His vision. Too many people claim to be about the Father's business when they are really only concerned with their own agenda. While others may not be able to recognize the difference, God looks at the heart.

As you pursue ministry, guard your heart and keep your focus on God. He's the one who rewards you and crowns your efforts with success. Don't delight yourself in the approval of man but in God's presence and in the joy that comes from knowing He is satisfied with you.

Reflect and Pray

Today I release any misguided intention I've attached to my desire to go after the things of God. In pursuing ministry, I won't let anything hinder me from serving humbly and authentically.

Lord, thank You for calling and choosing me for the ministry work You've assigned me to. Help me to do it in a way that allows others to see You in me and to feel the love of God every time they come into contact with me.

In Jesus' name, Amen.

Pursue Now

And he said to all, "If anyone would come after me, let him deny himself and take up his cross daily and follow me. For whoever would save his life will lose it, but whoever loses his life for my sake will save it.

Luke 9:23-24, ESV

Daughter of God, you've made it to the final devotion. And what a journey it's been.

As you read this final devotion, take time to appreciate how far you've come since you first began. Take time to bask in the progress you've made.

Being a daughter of God and leading a life that pleases and honors Him requires radical intentionality, especially when others around you don't share your conviction. You are capable. You are called. You were created for a time such as this and you're ready to step into it. You have what it takes to stand.

So get after it. Wake up every single day determined to boldly and passionately live out your purpose in God. Hold fast to your belief and stand on the Word of God without wavering. When you feel discouraged, remind yourself of who and whose you are. It won't be easy, but God is fighting for you, rooting for you to win and removing every hindrance that threatens your progress.

You've worked so hard to get here. You've worked so hard to become. To be. To learn. To grow. To change. To heal. Now you've arrived at the moment where preparation and destiny collide. You are free to go after the things of God with renewed joy, fervor, zeal, focus and clarity. You've waited long enough; now it's your time. It's your moment. Release any lingering doubts and be committed to the process.

You've always been worthy.

You've always been the one.

Daughter of God, go forth!

147

Acknowledgments

Thank you, Lord, for blessing me with the gift of writing and the honor of being assigned to write this book for Your daughters. Thank you that You have never left, failed, forgotten, or forsaken me. Thank you that I've always been Your daughter.

Thank you to my phenomenal husband for supporting and pushing me every step of the way, and for making sure I was able to finish writing this book, no matter what. Thank you for creating the most beautiful cover I could've imagined but couldn't articulate. I'm so grateful that God created you, just for me. Life with you is daily evidence of His favor concerning me. I'm so blessed to call you mine.

Thank you to my son, Shai, for just being you. You are perfect in every way. May you always know how loved you are.

Thank you to my amazing mom and sisters: Kathyrn, Katonya, Angela, and Karisha for being my core, for always seeing and believing in me, and for reminding me of who I am when I feel unsure. Thank you to my entire family for being in my corner and loving me endlessly.

Thank you to my incredible leaders, Apostle Ronald and Pastor LaShawn Demery, for creating a safe space, Christ Way Cathedral, for me to heal, learn, grow, and thrive. Thank you for praying for me, encouraging me, and pushing me toward my destiny. Thank you, Christ Way, for your unwavering support and constant kindness.

Thank you to Aunt Juan and my entire village for always stepping up and being so kind, helpful and giving.

Thank you to my friends: Akiras, Aniya, Asia, Brandi, Candace, Lartrice, and Rebekah for your push and your pour over the course of me writing and promoting this book.

Thank you to the launch team for getting the word out!

Thank you to every person who's been a part of my journey, no matter the role you played.

It was all worth it.

About
Kharis Publishing:

Kharis Publishing, an imprint of Kharis Media LLC, is a leading Christian and inspirational book publisher based in Aurora, Chicago metropolitan area, Illinois. Kharis' dual mission is to give voice to under-represented writers (including women and first-time authors) and equip orphans in developing countries with literacy tools. That is why, for each book sold, the publisher channels some of the proceeds into providing books and computers for orphanages in developing countries so that these kids may learn to read, dream, and grow. For a limited time, Kharis Publishing is accepting unsolicited queries for nonfiction (Christian, self-help, memoirs, business, health and wellness) from qualified leaders, professionals, pastors, and ministers. Learn more at: https://kharispublishing.com/